GET THE MOST FROM
PHOTOSHOP

GET THE MOST FROM
PHOTOSHOP

SIMON JOINSON

David and Charles

For Felix

A DAVID & CHARLES BOOK

David & Charles is an F&W Media Inc. company,
4700 East Galbraith Road
Cincinnati, OH 45236

First published in the UK in 2009

Text, design and illustrations
Copyright © Simon Joinson 2009

Simon Joinson has asserted his right to be
identified as author of this work in accordance
with the Copyright, Designs and Patents Act, 1988.

Adobe® and Photoshop® are either registered
trademarks or trademarks of Adobe Systems
Incorporated in the United States and/or other
countries. All other trademarks used are property
of their respective trademark owners.

A catalogue record for this book is available
from the British Library.

ISBN-13: 978-0-7153-2971-9 hardback
ISBN-10: 0-7153-2971-5 hardback
ISBN-13: 978-0-7153-2962-7 paperback
ISBN-10: 0-7153-2962-6 paperback

Printed in China by RR Donnelley
for David & Charles
Brunel House, Newton Abbot, Devon

Commissioning Editor   Neil Baber
Editor   Bethany Dymond
Project Editor   Ame Verso
Art Editor   Martin Smith
Production Controller   Kelly Smith

Visit our website at www.davidandcharles.co.uk

David & Charles books are available from all
good bookshops; alternatively you can contact
our Orderline on 0870 9908222 or write to us at
FREEPOST EX2 110, D&C Direct, Newton Abbot, TQ12
4ZZ (no stamp required UK only). US customers
call 800-289-0963 and Canadian customers call
800-840-5220.

CONTENTS

INTRODUCTION

I've heard it said that the average human only makes use of around 10 per cent of his or her brain power, and for most casual users the same applies to Adobe Photoshop. The undisputed big daddy of the image editing world, Photoshop has grown from relatively humble beginnings into the powerful, feature-laden behemoth it is today. This book isn't an attempt to rewrite the Photoshop manual, nor does it attempt to explain every single tool, menu item and option in excruciating detail. There are significant chunks of the program I'll only cover in passing detail (and many of the more esoteric or highly specialized functionality I've ignored entirely). This is because I didn't want to produce yet another Photoshop encyclopedia; I wanted to produce something the novice user can digest easily and,

crucially, apply what they learn to their own images by following the techniques in simple steps.

The first section of the book deals with Photoshop Basics; the things you need to grasp before you can take even the smallest first steps with your own pictures. We'll be covering essential tools and techniques and learning about non-destructive editing using Layers and Masks. As we move on to more specific techniques you'll find more and more step-by-step projects that you can follow with your own images (or, if you prefer, using the same images by downloading them from **www. getthemostfromphotoshop.com**).

Throughout the book you'll find hints and tips and keyboard shortcuts (see page 6), as well as suggestions for variations on the techniques that you can try on your own images.

Visit the website at **www.getthemostfromphotoshop.com** (or for the lazy typist, **www.gtmfp.net**) for links, image downloads and additional resources, as well as to put your questions about this book and its content to the author.

Photoshop is an amazingly powerful tool capable of transforming images in ways that would have been unimaginable in the days of the traditional darkroom. But it is just that, a tool: it doesn't have the 'lead you by the hand' ease of use of more consumer-friendly image-editing applications, nor does it offer much in the way of one-click fixes or enhancements. It's down to you, the user, to tame all that power and to learn - with help from this book of course - to get the most out of Photoshop.

I've been using Photoshop daily since 1992 and I can honestly say I'm still learning and discovering new techniques, new effects and new ways to save time or effort by doing the old things more efficiently. When I'm asked why I recommend Photoshop over other, less expensive applications I don't only point out the uniquely comprehensive toolset or the elegant, mature user interface. I also point out that Photoshop has far and away the largest community of active, enthusiastic users - both professional and amateur - who share their techniques and tips on countless websites, forums and magazine pages. This book will, I hope, be a springboard from which you can launch a long, fruitful relationship with this remarkable application.

Starting to learn Photoshop can be a daunting experience, and it's surprisingly easy to produce eye-wateringly awful results with only a few clicks of the mouse. But as you start to get a feel for the basic toolset you can stop worrying about *how* to use it and start thinking creatively about *what* you're trying to achieve. The necessary skills can be developed with practice, but ultimately it's your creative vision that will determine the success, or not, of your image editing.

Unusually, this book isn't specific to a particular version of Photoshop; virtually all the techniques and tools described are applicable to everything from Photoshop 7.0 right through to the very latest version. This is mainly because it concentrates mostly on techniques using the core tools that have been at the heart of the program for many years. Where there are differences, you'll find them clearly indicated in the text.

CHAPTER ONE
GETTING STARTED WITH PHOTOSHOP

Taking your first steps in Photoshop can be a daunting experience, but you'll find it a lot easier if you take a little time to find your way around the workspace and to familiarize yourself with the tools, dialogs and menus you'll be using as you start your journey into the world of advanced image editing.

Despite its ever-expanding feature set, many of the core tools and techniques of Photoshop haven't changed for many years. The most significant upgrade ever – to Photoshop 3.0, which introduced layers and tabbed palettes – was way back in 1994, and the most of the key tools of the versions covered in this book – 7.0 and the various Creative Suite (CS) incarnations – are functionally identical, even if the one you're using looks a little different or lacks some of the bells and whistles of latest version.

This chapter looks at Photoshop's workspace, menus, tools and palettes. Many of the techniques and step-by-step projects later in the book assume that you have a grasp of these Photoshop basics; using the menus and palettes, using sliders and previews, and knowing your way around the tool and Options bars. Unless you're a complete computer novice, most of this shouldn't be too challenging, but if the sum total of your previous software experience is sending a few emails and writing letters in Microsoft Word then be prepared for a steep learning curve to begin with.

It does get easier though; Photoshop's tools work in a consistent and relatively logical way, and it shouldn't be too long before you're transforming your images like a true pro.

Important note: CS3 introduced an extended version of Photoshop with advanced 3D, video and analysis tools. These additional features are outside the scope of this book and are not covered at all.

THE PHOTOSHOP WORKSPACE

Virtually every screenshot in this book features Photoshop CS3 running on Mac OS X. The version you're using may look different (particularly if you're on Windows XP or Vista), but under the skin the Photoshop workspace has remained remarkably consistent since version 7.0. There are five main constituents to Photoshop's workspace; the document window itself and the tool palette, Menu bar, tool Options bar, and the assortment of palettes you currently have open. I'll be referring to all these on a regular basis throughout the book, so take some time to familiarize yourself with the workspace of your particular version.

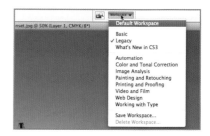

All versions of Photoshop allow you to save palette locations in different workspaces. More recent versions also have a selection of built-in Presets.

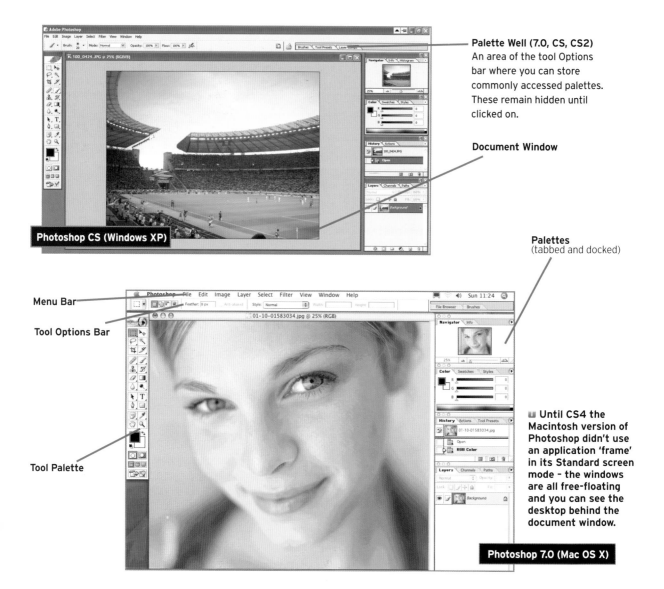

Photoshop CS (Windows XP)

Palette Well (7.0, CS, CS2)
An area of the tool Options bar where you can store commonly accessed palettes. These remain hidden until clicked on.

Document Window

Palettes
(tabbed and docked)

Menu Bar

Tool Options Bar

Tool Palette

⊞ **Until CS4 the Macintosh version of Photoshop didn't use an application 'frame' in its Standard screen mode – the windows are all free-floating and you can see the desktop behind the document window.**

Photoshop 7.0 (Mac OS X)

VIEW MODES

Photoshop offers three view modes (increased to four in version CS3); press the F key to cycle through them.

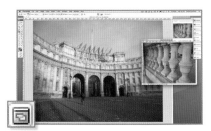

The **Standard** screen mode (the default) is the only 'windowed' view where you can have several images open in overlapping windows.

It looks a little different on a Windows computer, as Photoshop uses a grey background to fill the entire screen.

Full Screen with Menu Bar - useful for working on a single image. In Windows you can also click on an image window's **Maximize** button to have it fill all the available space.

Full Screen mode also gets rid of the menu bar, leaving only the tools and palettes (and the tool Options bar if turned on). The background colour turns black in this view mode.

CS3 added a fourth option: **Maximized**. In this mode the document window fills all available space between palettes and resizes when dock widths change. You also get scroll bars.

Press the Tab key to temporarily hide all open palettes and tools. You can right-click on the background colour to change it.

PHOTOSHOP MENUS

Photoshop's top-level menus are surprisingly simple - mainly because there's a lot of stuff hidden away in sub-menus and palettes. They're also remarkably logical - most things are where you'd expect them to be. If you do find the menus overwhelming and are using CS2 or later you can use **Edit>Menus** to hide menu items you're not going to use and even colour individual menu items to make them easier to navigate. Any changes you make

can be saved as a new Menu Set or as part of a custom Workspace (**Window>Workspace>Save Workspace**).

Layers, Filters and Selections get their own menus, and all the basic image adjustments (tone, size, rotation, cropping) and so on, are grouped together under the **Image** menu. The **Edit** menu

is home to a rather disparate collection of functions (some seemingly there simply because there's nowhere else for them) from the usual Cut, Copy and Paste, to Layer Transformations and Color Settings. Most (though not all) menu items have keyboard shortcuts (these are customizable via the **Edit** menu).

Adobe Photoshop

File   Edit   Image   Layer   Select   Filter   View   Window   Help

PHOTOSHOP PALETTES

Photoshop's palettes (found under the **Window** menu) are an essential part of the workspace and home to many of its most useful and powerful tools. Palettes can contain information (such as the Histogram and Info palettes) but most are interactive and contain sliders, buttons and other tools. All palettes are non-modal; you don't have to confirm any changes before you move on to doing something else, and all have their own flyout Options menus – just click on the little arrow at the top right of the panel. Most have additional options in context

menus – accessed by right-clicking on items in the palette.

Palettes can be grouped into single panels using tabs or locked together (docked) and can be collapsed and left open without getting in the way. Note that since Photoshop CS3, palettes have been called panels, though the two are still used interchangeably.

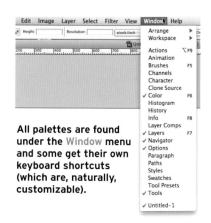

All palettes are found under the Window menu and some get their own keyboard shortcuts (which are, naturally, customizable).

Until Photoshop CS3's extensive user interface redesign, the tool Options bar was home to a Palette Well. Drag any palette here to add it and click on the tab to view the palette itself.

PALETTES/PANELS IN CS3 AND LATER

To save space, Photoshop CS3 uses palette docks and small icons, allowing lots of palettes to remain open without cluttering the screen.

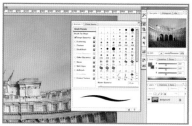

Individual palettes/panels remain docked when their icon is clicked on, but expand to full size so you can use them.

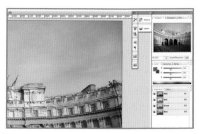

If you expand an entire dock, those to the left move to accommodate the expanded panels. Press Shift-Tab to toggle panel visibility.

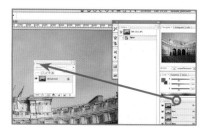

Individual palettes can be dragged off a docked pane (click on the palette name and drag) if you want to use one as a free-floating window.

Conversely, any palette can be added to a dock or panel by dragging it until you see the blue line (horizontal to add to a panel or dock, vertical to create a new dock).

Here are all the panels and palettes from the first screenshot expanded; as you can see, there's not a lot of room left for the picture I'm working on.

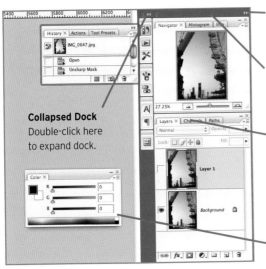

Expand/collapse Dock Button

Expanded Dock
Double-click here to collapse to icons.

Collapsed Dock
Double-click here to expand dock.

Panel of Tabbed Palettes
Double-click any palette name to minimize it.

Single Palette
Officially even single palettes are actually now called panels, but throughout the book I've stuck to the old terminology to make the distinction.

▲ **Palettes and panels (in any version of Photoshop) can be minimized by double-clicking the palette name.**

All palettes have flyout Options menus – click on the small arrow at the top left of the palette to activate it.

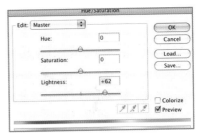

DIALOG BOXES

Photoshop has three basic dialog boxes (what you see when you choose a command from a menu). The first (such as Hue/Saturation) consists of one or more sliders and will usually offer several options menus and check boxes. To see the effect of your changes (where applicable) on the image itself make sure the Preview option is ticked – for before and after comparisons toggle the Preview on and off.

Most effect and filter dialogs have their own Preview windows – again there is check box to preview the effect on the actual image (though this will slow down the more complex filters). In all dialog boxes holding down the Alt (⌥) key turns the Cancel button into a Reset button.

▲ **Adjustments dialogs preview changes on the image itself.**

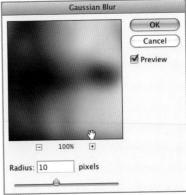

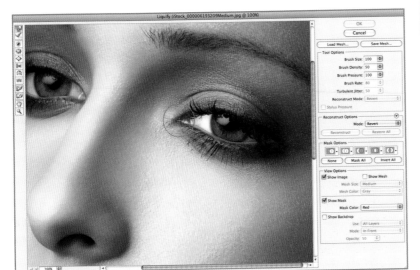

▲ **Always preview effects and filters at 100%. Click on Preview in the dialog to see the original image.**

◄ **Some complex filters have much larger dialogs with big Previews and lots of options.**

11

PHOTOSHOP TOOLS

For simple tonal corrections and filters, you'll only ever need a handful of Photoshop's array of tools – and most of those are the core Selection and Painting tools that have been around in one form or another since the program first appeared in the 1990s. Since those earliest days the tools have got a little more sophisticated, but it's surprising how little the tool palette has changed in the last decade. Below is a fully annotated diagram showing all the tools in Photoshop CS3 (the first version, incidentally, to allow you to use a tall thin tool palette – shown on the edge of the opposite page). Some of the tools below are covered in depth later in the book, others we're not going to touch at all.

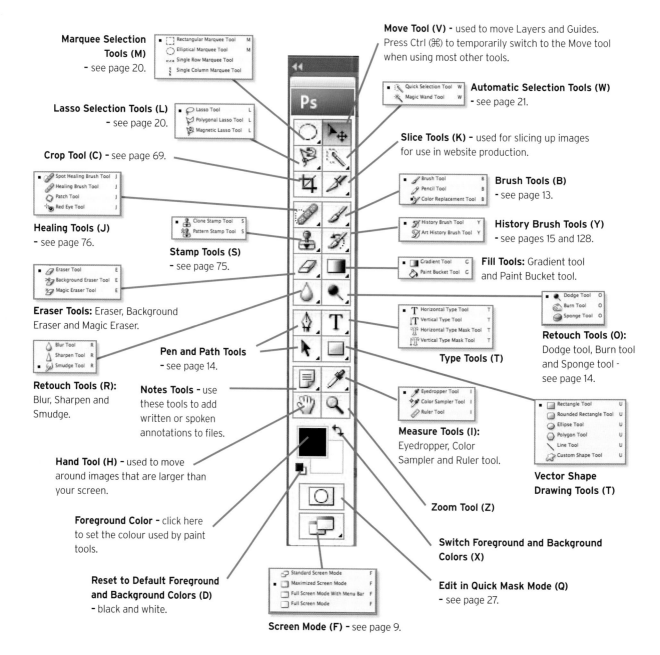

Marquee Selection Tools (M)
– see page 20.

Rectangular Marquee Tool M
Elliptical Marquee Tool M
Single Row Marquee Tool
Single Column Marquee Tool

Lasso Selection Tools (L)
– see page 20.

Lasso Tool L
Polygonal Lasso Tool L
Magnetic Lasso Tool L

Crop Tool (C) – see page 69.

Spot Healing Brush Tool J
Healing Brush Tool J
Patch Tool J
Red Eye Tool J

Healing Tools (J)
– see page 76.

Clone Stamp Tool S
Pattern Stamp Tool S

Stamp Tools (S)
– see page 75.

Eraser Tool E
Background Eraser Tool E
Magic Eraser Tool E

Eraser Tools: Eraser, Background Eraser and Magic Eraser.

Blur Tool R
Sharpen Tool R
Smudge Tool R

Retouch Tools (R): Blur, Sharpen and Smudge.

Pen and Path Tools
– see page 14.

Notes Tools – use these tools to add written or spoken annotations to files.

Hand Tool (H) – used to move around images that are larger than your screen.

Foreground Color – click here to set the colour used by paint tools.

Reset to Default Foreground and Background Colors (D)
– black and white.

Standard Screen Mode F
Maximized Screen Mode F
Full Screen Mode With Menu Bar F
Full Screen Mode F

Screen Mode (F) – see page 9.

Move Tool (V) – used to move Layers and Guides. Press Ctrl (⌘) to temporarily switch to the Move tool when using most other tools.

Quick Selection Tool W
Magic Wand Tool W

Automatic Selection Tools (W)
– see page 21.

Slice Tools (K) – used for slicing up images for use in website production.

Brush Tool B
Pencil Tool B
Color Replacement Tool B

Brush Tools (B)
– see page 13.

History Brush Tool Y
Art History Brush Tool Y

History Brush Tools (Y)
– see pages 15 and 128.

Gradient Tool G
Paint Bucket Tool G

Fill Tools: Gradient tool and Paint Bucket tool.

Horizontal Type Tool T
Vertical Type Tool T
Horizontal Type Mask Tool T
Vertical Type Mask Tool T

Type Tools (T)

Dodge Tool O
Burn Tool O
Sponge Tool O

Retouch Tools (O): Dodge tool, Burn tool and Sponge tool – see page 14.

Eyedropper Tool I
Color Sampler Tool I
Ruler Tool I

Measure Tools (I): Eyedropper, Color Sampler and Ruler tool.

Rectangle Tool U
Rounded Rectangle Tool U
Ellipse Tool U
Polygon Tool U
Line Tool U
Custom Shape Tool U

Vector Shape Drawing Tools (T)

Zoom Tool (Z)

Switch Foreground and Background Colors (X)

Edit in Quick Mask Mode (Q)
– see page 27.

Most of the tools on the tool palette have several sub-tools - click and hold the mouse down and they will appear. You can also hold down the Alt/⌥ key as you click on a tool to cycle through the various options (holding the Shift key when pressing a tool's keyboard shortcut does the same thing). Many of the tools are brushes of some type (see below), and all such tools act in the same way. You can vary the Brush Size (diameter in pixels), Opacity and Hardness (the lower the hardness the softer the edge of the brush) using the tool Options and brushes Presets - or via keyboard shortcuts ([and] alter size - Shift-[and Shift-] alter hardness).

All tools have their own specific options too, accessed via the tool Options bar that sits just below the main Menu bar - and you can save tool Presets for future use in the same place. Finally, many tools gain added functionality when used with a pressure-sensitive drawing tablet - great if you're better with a pencil than a mouse.

QUICK GUIDE TO BRUSHES

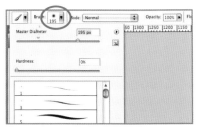

The basic options for any painting tool are the same and are found in the tool **Options** bar. Here you'll also find lots of Preset brushes to play with.

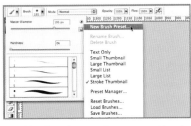

Use the flyout menu to save and load brush **Presets** and to change the way they are displayed.

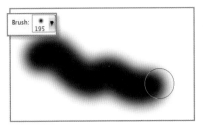

The **Brush Size** defines the width of the stroke in pixels. Here, I'm using a large brush with a low **Hardness** setting (for a soft edge).

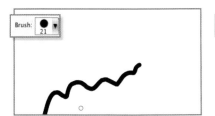

The Hardness setting defines the feathering of the edge of the stroke. Here's a small Size with a high (100%) Hardness setting.

The **Opacity** defines how much paint is laid down in a single stroke - the transparency. Multiple strokes will add to any previous paint.

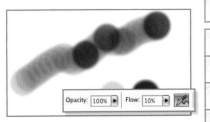

Click on the **Airbrush** icon and you can change the **Flow** setting - this varies the Opacity according to how fast you move the brush.

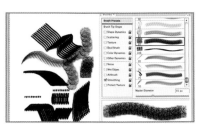

The **Brushes** palette (Window> Brushes) has more options for **Brush Dynamics** - many related to the use of a pressure-sensitive pen.

You can create your own brushes by copying a square area from an image you've created, and choosing **Edit>Define Brush Preset**.

One handy use for this is to create your own copyright brush for one-click watermarking of your photos.

There are some tools you may never use; the Pen tool, for example, is notoriously difficult for master for anyone without a graphic design background, and the Blur and Sharpen tools do nothing you can't achieve more efficiently using Layers and Masks. But one of the defining characteristics of Photoshop is that there are many different ways to do the same thing, and you may well end up using tools I haven't clicked on for years.

Whenever you're using a tool make sure you check out its Options as these can often significantly change the way they operate (use **Window>Options** to make the Options bar visible if you can't see it).

OTHER USEFUL TOOLS

The **Burn** tool darkens tones – you can restrict the effect to the shadows, highlights or mid-tones using the tool Options bar.

The **Dodge** tool does the opposite; it lightens tones. Use the Dodge and Burn tools to increase contrast locally and to fix lighting problems.

The **Sponge** tool lets you paint saturation changes (choose **Saturate** or **Desaturate** from the Options bar). Great for toning down red skin.

Quick Tips

■ Hold down the Shift key and right-click when using any Painting tool to change the paint Blending Mode. Right-click (without the Shift key) to bring up the Brush Size and Hardness sliders.

■ Press the Alt (⌥) key while using Paint or Fill tools to temporarily activate the Eyedropper tool (used to set the Foreground Color).

■ Press the Alt (⌥) key while using the Dodge tool to temporarily switch to the Burn tool (and vice versa). The Alt (⌥) key switches between saturating and desaturating when using the Sponge tool and switches between the Blur and Sharpen tools.

■ The Shift key constrains painting tools to perfectly straight horizontal, or vertical lines (and keeps Marquee selections perfectly square too).

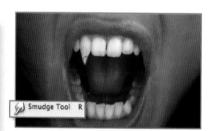

The **Smudge** tool does what its name suggests, pushing pixels around as if they are wet paint. It can be useful for awkward blending jobs.

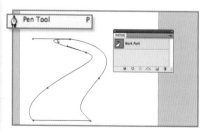

The **Pen** tool is used to create resolution-independent **Paths**. If you're an Illustrator, you may find Paths easier than freehand drawing.

There are a couple of automatic erasers – this is the one-click **Magic Eraser** tool. It's a combination of the Magic Wand and the Delete key.

The most common use for the Pen tool is to create selections around awkward subjects. Paths can easily be turned into selections and vice versa.

GETTING STARTED:
KEY TOOLS: HISTORY

A powerful, versatile and sophisticated tool for moving backwards and forwards through the stages of your work.

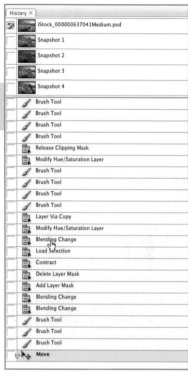

Photoshop's History feature is a powerful tool that builds on the concept of multiple Undos to offer a sophisticated way of turning back time.

Every time you do anything to your image, Photoshop creates a History State, up to the maximum number defined in the program's Preferences (after which it forgets the oldest step to make way for the latest). These States can be used in several ways. The first is a simple multiple Undo; press

Ctrl-Alt-Z (⌘-⌥-Z) to take a step backwards, Ctrl-Shift-Z (⌘-⇧-Z) to step forwards. Individual History States can also be selected by clicking on them in the History palette (**Window>History**). The History palette also allows you to record the nature of a document at a specific moment in time by saving a Snapshot, so you can go back to it at any point in the future. Finally the History Brush tool lets you paint with a chosen History State or Snapshot.

▲ **The History palette showing several Snapshots and the last 23 States.**

Quick Tips

■ History States are not saved with images after you close them, so create new documents if you want to save your work in several States.

■ To create a new document from any State or Snapshot, right-click and choose **New Document** from the menu that appears.

■ **Non-Linear History** (one of the Options) is more flexible but many users find it confusing (it allows you to go back to an earlier State, edit the document, and yet still see the subsequent steps in the History palette).

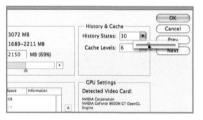

The number of States Photoshop remembers is set using the **Performance** tab of the **Preferences** dialog. Be aware that more States mean more memory is being used.

You can create new **Snapshots** whenever you want (but remember each uses a lot of disk space).

A new State is created every time you perform an edit on the document (however, if you Undo an edit it won't be recorded).

The History palette's Options are fairly simple. Without **Allow Non-Linear History** selected, editing after selecting a previous State deletes all subsequent States.

USING THE HISTORY FUNCTION

The History functions aren't only for retracing your steps when things go wrong; they also have some cool creative uses too. Here's a quick primer on History essentials.

Before you make any major changes to your document create a new **Snapshot** using the History palette's pop-out menu.

You can name the Snapshot if you want. You'll normally want to create the Snapshot from the **Full Document**.

The new Snapshot appears at the top of the History palette. You can now carry on editing the image (here, turning it to black and white).

At any point you can go back to a previous State by simply clicking on it in the History palette. Newer States are 'greyed out', but still selectable.

Clicking in the little box to the left of a state (or Snapshot) sets the **Source** for the History Brush.

Select the **History Brush** tool and you can now paint with the State selected in the last step – painting with Undo.

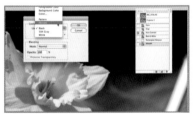

The **Fill** command (**Edit>Fill**) also has the option to use the currently selected History Source.

Here, I've made a rectangular selection, feathered it and filled with History.

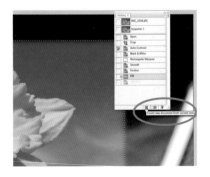

You can turn any state or Snapshot into a new document by clicking on the left icon at the bottom of the History palette (the other two are **New Snapshot** and **Delete State/Snapshot**). Note that the document created needs to be saved if you want to keep it.

▲ When painting with the History Brush you can change the Source State at any point. This makes it easy to correct any mistakes you make while painting with History – simply choose a Source State before the point in the project where you made the mistake.

VERSION DIFFERENCES

Despite the fact that every new Photoshop version brings a raft of new features, for the purposes of the techniques and tools discussed in this book the differences in many cases are largely cosmetic.

Virtually all the screenshots are taken from CS3, which saw a fairly major redesign of the user interface (something that's happened again in CS4 - see page 18), but at a glance versions 7.0, CS and CS2 look remarkably similar. On this page I've tried to list all the key version changes that will make a difference to the non-professional user (and those that involve tools covered in this book).

Introduced in Photoshop CS
- Camera Raw Plug-In (page 156)
- Interactive Histogram Palette
- Shadow/Highlight Adjustment (page 53)
- Lens Blur Filter (pages 104-105 and 135)
- Photo Filter Adjustment (page 63)
- Filter Gallery (page 126-127)
- Custom Keyboard Shortcuts (page 158)
- Layer Comps (page 145)
- Color Match and Color Replace Tools

Introduced in Photoshop CS2
- Bridge (page 153-155)
- Smart Sharpen (page 66)
- Warp Transformations (page 141)

- Spot Heal and Red-Eye Tools (pages 76 and 84)
- Noise Reduction Filter (page 86)
- Smart Objects (pages 36 and 81)
- Multiple Layer Select (page 144)
- Lens Correction Filter (page 111)
- Custom Menus (page 9)
- Shape Blur, Surface Blur, Box Blur

Introduced in Photoshop CS3
- New Interface with Docks (page 10)
- Camera Raw 4 (page 156)
- Upgraded Curves Dialog (page 54)
- Smart Filters (page 67)
- Black and White Adjustment (page 97)
- Layer Alignment Tool
- Quick Selection Tool (page 21)

- Refine Edge (page 26)
- Bridge 2.0 (page 154)

Introduced in Photoshop CS4
- New Workspace and Interface (page 18)
- Tabbed Document Windows
- Upgraded, Faster Bridge (page 155)
- Adjustments Panel (pages 18 and 46)
- Masks Panel (pages 18 and 42)
- Extensive Adjustments Presets
- Vibrance Adjustment (page 62)
- On-Image Controls for Hue/Saturation, Curves and Other Adjustments (page 96)
- Camera Raw 5.0 with Selective Image Editing (page 156)
- Improved Dodge, Burn and Sponge Tools

Setting-Up Photoshop

Photoshop can be tailored to the needs of the individual user in many ways - from the appearance of the workspace to the keyboard shortcuts and menus. The application Preferences (Edit>Preferences on Windows, Photoshop>Preferences on a Macintosh) are for more fundamental options and generally you can leave them at their default installation settings.

Depending on the version you're using the **Preferences** dialog will have up to ten pages of options. The only ones I'd worry about are **Displays** and **Cursors** (make sure the Brush Size option is checked

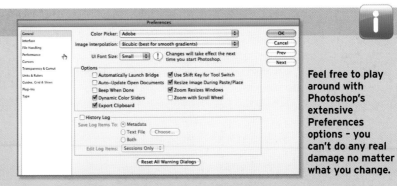

Feel free to play around with Photoshop's extensive Preferences options - you can't do any real damage no matter what you change.

for Painting Cursors), **Units & Rulers** (I tend to use Pixels for all Units), **Plug-Ins** and **Scratch Disks**. The latter allows you to set any disk attached to your computer as a scratch disk, used by Photoshop to store the immense temporary files it creates as you work. A large, fast scratch disk (separate from

the disk your operating system and Photoshop itself reside on) can make a huge difference to the speed and stability of Photoshop if you regularly work with large files. This - along with adding more RAM to your machine - is one of the easiest, most effective ways to improve Photoshop's performance.

PHOTOSHOP CS4: WHAT'S NEW?

When I started work on this book Photoshop CS3 was relatively new, by the time I finished it CS4 was well on the way to announcement. Photoshop CS4 sees a further refinement of the significant interface changes introduced in CS3 (including, for the first time, an application frame for Macintosh users). Many of the workspace changes are cosmetic, some (such as tabbed document windows and the new App bar) have a more fundamental effect on the way we interact with Photoshop. Under the hood there are some fairly serious changes, including 64-bit native operation (Windows only) and boosted graphics performance for those with the right GPU hardware, providing amongst other things, stepless smooth zooming, view rotation and 'pick and flick' image scrolling.

There are a couple of important new palettes; the Adjustments panel creates Adjustment Layers in a single click and allows you to change the adjustment settings directly from the panel (rather than using a modal dialog). The panel also gives access to a wide range of Presets for each adjustment, which makes

Photoshop CS4 sees another fairly significant refinement of the Photoshop user interface. New features include the App Bar (on windows this is incorporated into the menu bar), tabbed document windows and - for Macintosh users - an application frame that keeps everything neatly together.

experimentation a lot easier. The new Masks panel gives you non-destructive feathering of masks (and the ability to reduce the density of the mask).

On the tools side of things there have been some enhancements to the Rubber Stamp and Healing tools' Clone Source option (which can now be clipped to the area covered by the brush in use).

Overall, the intentions with CS4 - aside from graphics acceleration and an improved

user interface - appear to be to reduce the need to use menus, to make it easier to dive in and start editing images, and to encourage non-destructive editing and experimentation through the use of Adjustment Layers and one-click Presets. At the time of writing Photoshop CS4 was still in closed beta, so what I've seen so far could well be fine-tuned before the final release. What I have seen however is impressive enough to consider this version a major landmark in Photoshop's 15-year history.

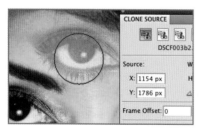

In Photoshop CS3 the Clone Overlay showed the entire image, which could be confusing.

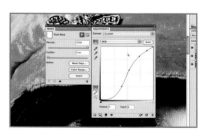

In CS4 you can choose to clip the Overlay so you can see exactly what you are going to paint. Very cool.

The Adjustments and Masks panels are major new features that will enhance everyone's workflow.

CHAPTER TWO
PHOTOSHOP BASICS
WORKING WITH SELECTIONS

Getting to grips with the tools for creating and modifying selections is the key to advanced Photoshop techniques. Accurate selections allow you to produce convincing montages, seamless localized colour corrections and eye-catching special effects. This chapter looks at what selections are, what they do and how to use them.

When you want to make a section of text in a document bold, italic, bigger or smaller, you highlight the words you want to change before doing anything. This lets the word processor know that you only want to change that particular section – be it a single word or an entire page.

In Photoshop the same principle applies, although now you're selecting groups of pixels not words, so you can isolate the particular area of the canvas you want to make changes to.

Photoshop offers a wide variety of Selection tools – most are common to all versions (and some go right back to the very earliest versions), although some, such as the

Magnetic Lasso, have arrived more recently. The number and variation of Selection tools – and tools for refining and modifying selections once they've been made – has been growing steadily over the last few years and in the latest CS versions of Photoshop you'll find a rather bewildering array of options.

This chapter concentrates on the most useful tools, and you'll find more information, tips and tricks on making and refining selections as you work your way through the step-by-step projects later in the book. You'll also learn that mastering the basic Selection tools is only the beginning, and that the real power lies in the alter ego of selections: masks.

PHOTOSHOP BASICS:
SELECTIONS AND SELECTION TOOLS

No matter what you want to do in Photoshop, at some point – probably very early on – you'll need to make a selection, so let's take a look at the various tools on offer.

Selections isolate groups of pixels - once you've made a selection, any subsequent actions (copying for example, or modifying the image by applying an effects filter) will only affect the pixels inside the selected area. Masks are examined in detail in the next chapter, but it's worth pointing out now that selections and masks are essentially the same thing; they're just presented and manipulated in a different way. A selection can be turned into a mask and a mask into a selection. Unlike a mask, a selection is a temporary thing (which is lost when you

SELECTION TOOLS

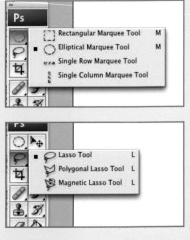

The Selection tools are grouped into three sections on Photoshop's tool palette. First come the Marquee tools (keyboard shortcut: M). To create a perfect square or circle hold down the Shift key while using the Rectangular or Elliptical tools.

Next are the three Lasso tools (keyboard shortcut: L), used to draw freehand selections (though one, the Magnetic Lasso, automatically 'snaps' to any nearby edge). The Polygonal Lasso is used to create straight lines.

Finally come the Magic Wand and the Quick Selection tool (CS3 and later). These tools make selections based on colour and can be a very useful and quick way to select areas of an image automatically (see opposite).

▼ Selections are shown on screen by an animated line of 'marching ants'.

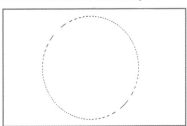

▼ Any tool or effect you use (here, it's a simple paintbrush) will only affect the pixels inside the selected area.

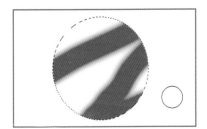

close the file, for example) - if you save a selection (**Select>Save Selection...**) Photoshop simply creates a mask and hides it away as an extra channel.

There are three basic types of Selection tool in Photoshop (see above) - simple, geometric shapes (squares and circles), freehand selections (those you draw yourself) and automatic tools that

select groups of pixels of the same - or similar - colour/brightness (the Magic Wand and - in CS3/CS4 - the Quick Selection tool). Selections can also be created using the **Select>Color Range** menu item (which allows you, as the name implies, to select all pixels of a particular colour, with user-definable Tolerance options). As we'll see later, you can also

AUTOMATIC SELECTION TOOLS

The Magic Wand (and the new Quick Selection tool) and the Magnetic Lasso are designed to take some of the effort out of the process of making selections; here's how they work.

The basic principle of the Magic Wand is simple; it selects areas based on colour. The **Tolerance** setting defines how wide the range of colours is that will be included in the selection.

Clicking anywhere in the flower shape selects the entire area. In a simple case such as this there is little or no variance in colour in the area we want to select.

The Magnetic Lasso is a freehand Selection tool that finds edges and 'snaps' the selection to them. There are options for how close an edge must be to the cursor (the **Width** setting) and how well defined an edge must be for the selection to follow it (the **Contrast** setting).

CS3's Quick Selection tool is Photoshop's most automatic Selection tool yet. It works in a similar way to the Magic Wand, but is used more like a brush, gradually adding to the selection as you drag it around the image.

create selections based on the transparency of a particular layer or Channel and - as mentioned at the start of this section - you can create selections from masks.

Finally, Photoshop offers various tools to refine and modify the selections you've made, and to use the tools to add to or remove from existing selections.

Smart Selections

Whether you're using the automatic Selection tools or not, the more you use Photoshop the more tricks you'll pick up for making accurate selections in the most efficient way. The easiest way to cut out a complex object, for example, is to think the other way around; use the Magic Wand to select everything except the object then invert the selection (**Select>Inverse**). Or, as the example on the right shows, you can combine different tools using the add (Shift key) or subtract (Alt/⬸ key) modes.

It's also important to start to understand what the various options for each tool do. This is particularly true of the Magic Wand and Magnetic Lasso, which both have settings that significantly change the way they work. There are a few options

Start by using the Rectangular Marquee to draw a box around the object (in this case the man).

Now, select the Magic Wand and hold down the Alt (⬸) key. Click on the sand inside the rectangular selection you just made to subtract these pixels from the selection.

Selection Mode

Add, Replace or Take Away
Photoshop allows you to choose how Selection tools work when you already have an active selection. There are three basic options; **New Selection** (the new selection replaces the existing one). This is the default setting. The other two are **Add** and **Subtract**, which do exactly what their names imply – new selections are either added to or taken away from the existing selection.

The Add mode is invoked by holding down the Shift key when using the tool, and the Subtract mode by holding down the Alt (✎) key, though you can fix the mode by clicking on the relevant icon in the Options bar. Incidentally, there is a fourth option, **Intersect**, which leaves only the overlap between existing and new selections.

common to most of the Selection tools; the Anti Alias option is normally left checked at all times (without it you'll get jagged edges to selections with curves or diagonal lines in them).

Likewise, the Feather option is normally left on zero. This option allows you to add a soft (feathered) edge to any selection you make – most people prefer to do this in a separate step (**Select>Feather** or **Select>Modify >Feather...**) – see page 24 – simply because you can't preview the effect of feathering, so if you decide you used too much or too little the only option is to start again from scratch.

Photoshop CS3's Quick Selection tool (which acts like a Magic Wand but is used like a brush) has only one option: Auto-Enhance, which attempts to refine the edges of any selections it makes.

Transforming Selections

It's rare that your first attempt at anything other than the most basic selection will be right first time. Fortunately, there are many ways to fine-tune or refine your selections – we'll look at them in depth over the page. Before that, it's worth mentioning that you can transform a selection, which in Photoshop speak means you can scale it, stretch it, distort it flip it or even rotate it. Simply choose the **Select>Transform Selection** menu option and use the distortion handles that appear around the selection.

As with all Photoshop's distortion tools, right-clicking on any of the handles brings up a menu of options as shown below.

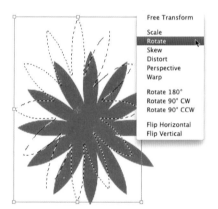

MAGIC WAND TOLERANCE

To understand Tolerance settings take a look at these two examples. With a low Tolerance setting only pixels very near the colour of the point clicked on are selected.

A higher Tolerance casts a much wider net and selects pixels of more varying colour. It's a fine balance and you usually need to experiment with the settings to get the result you're looking for.

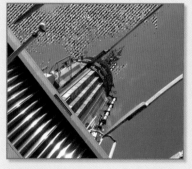

▲ Tolerance = 8

▲ Tolerance = 64

MAGIC WAND OPTIONS

As with all Selection tools, the Magic Wand has various options that control how it works. The most important is the Tolerance setting. Tolerance defines how wide the range of colours is that will be included in the selection. A low Tolerance selects adjacent pixels only if they are very close to the colour of the point you clicked on. Conversely, higher Tolerances select adjacent pixels that vary increasingly in colour.

Tolerance

Photoshop offers Tolerance settings of 0-255. At the zero setting, only pixels of exactly the same colour as the point you click will be selected. At 255 the whole image will be selected. A good starting point is 16 to 40.

Contiguous

When this option is ticked the tool will only select adjacent pixels (within the Tolerance setting) - when it's off the tool selects all pixels of the right colour across the entire image - even those nowhere near where you clicked.

Sample/Use All Layers

Uncheck this option if you want to restrict the effect of the Magic Wand selection to the layer that you are currently working on. If it is ticked it will sample from the entire image - all layers.

THE MAGNETIC LASSO

This tool attempts to find edges as you draw a selection, adding anchor points along the way, and it's a very useful tool once you've got to grips with it.

Start by clicking on the image to set the first anchor point. Now start drawing with the cursor.

Follow the edge you want to select as closely as possible. The Magnetic Lasso will create anchors along the way (you can also do it yourself by clicking).

When you get back to the start the cursor will change and the last click will create the selection.

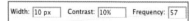

The Magnetic Lasso has three main options: **Width** (how far it looks for an edge) - if you've got a steady hand use a low setting; **Contrast** (how different two areas need to be to be considered an edge), and **Frequency** (how often the anchor points are added). You can delete the last anchor added using the Backspace key.

Top Tip

Sample Size

It's a little known fact that the Eyedropper tool is linked to the Magic Wand. Armed with this knowledge users can fine-tune even further the way the Magic Wand works.

First, select the Eyedropper tool (keyboard shortcut: I).

Now go to the tool Options bar and change the Sample Size setting. By default it is set to Point Sample. At this setting the Magic Wand behaves normally.

Try changing it to 3 by 3 or 5 by 5 Average and return to the Magic Wand (press W). You'll find it's much more forgiving of noisy areas or areas of slightly varying tone. The reason is that the Magic Wand normally uses the colour of a single pixel, with the Tolerance defining how near neighbouring pixels need to be (in colour terms) to be included in the selection. By increasing the Sample Size you are defining an average of 9 or 25 pixels with the first click.

Modifying Selections

No matter which tool you use, the chances are you'll need to fine-tune the selection, particularly if you're doing montage work or anything else that needs pixel-perfect accuracy. Photoshop provides a range of tools for refining selections in the **Select** menu (see right). **All** and **Deselect** are fairly straightforward, as are **Reselect** (brings back the last selection made) and **Inverse** (which flips the selection so everything that wasn't selected is, and vice versa). **Color Range...**, **Refine Edge...** (CS3 and later) and **Modify** are covered in more detail later (see pages 25-27), which just leaves **Grow** and **Similar**. These use the Magic Wand's current settings to expand the selection based on the colour and tonal values of the pixels inside your current selection. **Grow** selects all adjacent pixels of a similar colour, **Similar** selects any pixels in the entire image that are close enough in colour and tone. You can use these commands as many times as you need to gradually build up the selection you're after.

Now, let's look in a little more detail at some of those other selection modification options.

FEATHERING

Here's a very rough selection drawn around this helicopter using the **Polygonal Lasso**.

Using **Quick Mask mode** (see page 27) to view the selection as a coloured overlay, you can see more clearly the hard-edged shape drawn.

If you now copy and paste these pixels into a new image the join is obvious; the hard-edged selection makes sure of that.

Starting with the same selection now choose **Select>Modify> Feather...** and enter a **Feather Radius** of 30 pixels.

Now the selection looks very different when viewed as a mask. Just how large and soft the edge is depends on the Feather Radius you enter.

And now when you paste it into a new image it's far harder to see the join. You don't always need complex selections for effective montage.

SMOOTHING

Automatic Selection tools such as the Magic Wand can often produce rather messy results - smoothing is a great way to fill in the holes.

Here's a selection created by the **Magic Wand** - the combination of noise and the texture of the road has left lots of holes in the selection.

You can see this more clearly when the selected pixels are deleted. There's a mess of leftover spots and dots.

Tool Shortcuts
Most tools have a single letter shortcut. For tools that are grouped together, use the Shift key and the letter to cycle between them:

Marquee   **M**
(⇧-**M** *to cycle tools*)

Lasso, Magnetic Lasso   **L**
and Polygonal Lasso
(⇧-**L** *to cycle tools*)

Magic Wand and   **W**
Quick Selection Tool
(⇧-**W** *to cycle tools*)

Let's go back to the original selection and choose **Select>Modify>Smooth...**, entering a **Radius** of 2 or 3 pixels.

Now when you delete the selected pixels there are no holes - and the jagged edges are now smooth.

Other Useful Shortcuts
To temporarily switch between the standard and Polygonal Lasso tools while making a selection, hold down the alt key. This also works when using the Magnetic Lasso (temporarily switches to the Polygonal Lasso).

Invert Selection	Feather Selection

To add to a selection, hold down the Shift key, to subtract from a selection use the Alt (⧉) key.

EXPANDING AND CONTRACTING SELECTIONS

By default, tools such as the **Magic Wand** go right to an edge. But with ill-defined edges this can produce less than perfect results.

Choosing **Select>Modify>Expand...** allows you to grow the selection by however many pixels you want.

The **Contract...** option - useful for removing white fringes in situations such as this - shrinks the selection by however many pixels you tell it to.

SAVING SELECTIONS

If you've been working hard on a selection it might make sense to save it. Choose **Select>Save Selection...** and give it a name.

If you look at the **Channels** palette (**Window>Channels**) you'll see an extra channel has appeared for each selection you've saved.

You can recall the selection at any time using the **Select>Load Selection...** menu. You can even load selections from other open images.

Refine Edge (CS3+)

Photoshop CS3 introduced a neat new way to fine-tune the edge of your selections. Choosing the Refine Edge (**Select>Refine Edge**) menu (or clicking on the button in the Options bar) brings up a new dialog box with sliders for the various modification tools.

The Radius setting defines the size of the region around the selection boundary the edge refinement will work on. The Contrast setting sharpens up fuzzy edges and the Smooth, Feather and Contract/Expand sliders do the same thing as the menu tools. The big difference is you can combine them all and see the effect in a customizable Preview, which is shown below.

The five selection preview icons allow you to choose how you view the effect of your changes.

Press F to cycle through the preview options, press X to temporarily disable the preview and see the whole image.

SELECTING BY COLOUR RANGE

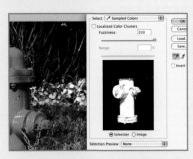

The **Select>Color Range...** option is useful for situations when you want to select only pixels of a specific colour.

When the dialog opens, click on the colour you want to select. The **Fuzziness** slider defines how wide the colour range is that is selected.

Click OK and you can now change the colour of all those pixels in seconds (here using the Hue/Saturation control - see pages 60-61).

Quick Mask Mode

The Quick Mask mode is one of Photoshop's most useful Selection tools, and for the advanced user is without a doubt the single most useful tool for fine-tuning existing selections. You'll find it used in virtually every project in the second half of this book, yet few new users ever go near it.

The basic idea behind the Quick Mask tool is simple. As mentioned earlier and covered in detail later, selections and masks are essentially interchangeable - when you make a selection everything outside the selection is masked. Quick Mask mode allows you to view - and crucially to edit - your selection as a mask. This means you can use Photoshop's full arsenal of brushes, filters and tonal controls to create pixel-perfect selections that simply aren't possible using the standard Selection tools alone.

Because you can see the mask (as a coloured overlay) it's also a lot easier to work with semi-

Quick Mask mode allows you to use brushes to paint selections using a temporary mask.

transparent (partial) selections - such as feathered edges - in Quick Mask mode, whereas in a standard selection there is a 50% cut-off point for the line of 'marching ants' - any pixels that are selected at below 50% will be left outside the selection border display (this doesn't mean they're not selected, they're just not shown as being inside the selection boundary, which can cause confusion).

To edit a selection in Quick Mask mode simply press the Q key. You'll see the Quick Mask overlay appear immediately.

Quick Mask Tips

■ Remember that (in its default mode) the coloured areas of the Quick Mask indicate the areas outside the selection - i.e. those areas that are masked.

■ You can view the Quick Mask channel without the image by pressing the Tilde (~) key.

■ To create an inverted Quick Mask from a selection hold down the Alt (⌥) key while clicking the Quick Mask icon on the tool palette.

■ You don't need to start with a selection; you can jump straight into Quick Mask mode and start painting. Black paint adds to the mask, white removes pixels and grey produces partially selected areas.

■ Any tool you can use on an image can be used on a Quick Mask; running a Blur filter on the mask, for example, produces an effect similar to feathering the selection.

■ Get into the habit of hitting the Q key every now and again when making complex selections - it's the easiest and most accurate way of checking how things are going.

REFINING SELECTIONS WITH QUICK MASK MODE

Start with a selection – here, I've used the **Magnetic Lasso** to draw around the bird quickly.

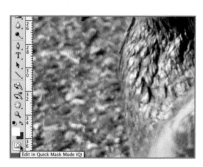

Switch to Quick Mask mode by pressing Q or by clicking on the **Edit in Quick Mask Mode** icon on the tool palette.

You can now see the mask created by your selection. Red areas are outside the selection, clear areas inside.

You can paint directly on to the Quick Mask using the standard paintbrush. Black paint adds to the mask (the red area) and white paint removes pixels from the mask (expands the selection).

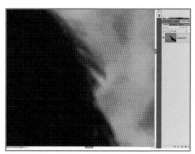

Using a very small brush allows you to create pixel-perfect selections. Use the X key to switch between black and white paint colours and the square brackets to change brush size.

When you're done simply press the Q key again to turn the Quick Mask back into a standard selection. Note, you can create Quick Mask selections from scratch too.

Quick Mask Options ⓘ

Double-clicking on the Quick Mask icon at the bottom of the tool palette lets you change a couple of options. One is the mask **Color** and **Opacity**, the other defines whether coloured areas show the selected parts or the unselected (masked) parts of the frame. The latter is the default, but you may find it more intuitive to switch. Note that throughout this book we're using Quick Mask in its default mode.

By default the overlay is red in masked areas (i.e. outside the selection) and clear in areas inside the selection, but you can change this using the Quick Mask Options (see left). Once you've finished editing the mask you can turn it back into a selection by simply pressing Q again.

We'll cover lots of different uses for Quick Mask mode as we work through the step-by-step projects later in the book but for now check out the quick walk-through at the top of this page, and have a play with it yourself – you'll soon wonder how you ever did without it.

Selections and Masks

Quick Masks are a powerful way to make pixel-level selections, but like selections, they are only temporary. To really start to use the power of masking for more complex work you need to get to grips with Layer Masks, and so that's where we're headed next in our journey through Photoshop.

CHAPTER THREE
PHOTOSHOP BASICS
LAYERS AND MASKS

Now that you've got the hang of selections and tried your hand at Quick Mask mode it's time to get serious with Photoshop's editing power tools. Mastering Layers and Masks is a key part of non-destructive editing and forms the ground rock for everything we're going to do from here on.

Until Layers arrived in image-editing applications all digital images were flat - if you placed an element from one image on top of another one, the new pixels replaced the original underlying pixels. If you wanted to go back later and make changes to the composition you were stuck. Layers - as the name suggests - allow you to build up an image in layers, with each one independently editable.

Each layer can contain a combination of opaque, transparent or semi-transparent pixels. Opaque pixels obscure anything on lower layers, while semi-transparent or transparent areas allow some - or all - of the pixels in underlying layers to show through. This chapter starts by looking at the very basic things you'll need to know to get started using Layers - how to create them, manipulate them and how to change how they interact with the other layers in the image 'stack'.

It then moves on to Layer Masks - these allow you to hide parts of a layer without actually removing the pixels - the key to non-destructive image manipulation.

It is safe to say that a mastery of layering is not only vital to effective digital image manipulation - it is the single most important thing you can learn.

PHOTOSHOP BASICS:
INTRODUCTION TO LAYERS

Layers are one of the most powerful and versatile tools in the digital darkroom. The next few pages look at how they work and how to use them.

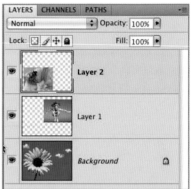

A single Photoshop file can contain anything from one to many thousands of layers (though each one increases the file size, so you'd never work with that many). The layers can be larger or smaller than the image Canvas Size, and their order can be changed by dragging them up or down the stack in the Layers palette.

If you take a pair of scissors and carefully cut a person out of one print and lay it on top of another print - a nice landscape for example - you know full well that the part of the image underneath the cut-out has not disappeared, it is merely hidden. And yet before the advent of Layers in digital-imaging applications, that was exactly what happened when attempting a digital montage.

Cutting part of one image and pasting it into another one permanently replaced one set of pixels with another. If you wanted to move the element you'd pasted at a later point you were stuck. This made digital montage a rather painful process - you had one chance to position each element correctly and if you decided the composition was wrong you simply started again. Layers changed all this. Not only did each element in a montage remain independent in its own layer, but you could alter the transparency of each layer, move and resize layers at will, and experiment with different Blending Modes. Although the most obvious use for Layers is when combining images into a montage it most certainly doesn't stop there.

▼ Any layer can contain transparent areas. Photoshop shows transparent areas with nothing below them in the layer stack using a grey checkerboard pattern.

Because you can duplicate all or part of a single image into a new layer, it is possible to experiment with different colour or tonal adjustments without ever having to commit to any changes and permanently alter the original until you are ready to.

In Photoshop the whole business of layering centres around the Layers palette

(**Window>Layers**, or press F7). From here you can hide or show individual layers, change Blending Modes, re-order the layer stack, group layers, delete them, change their Opacity, add Layer Masks and much more. You can find out more about the Layers palette on page 35 – for now just make sure you can find it and have it on-screen at all times.

You can find out more about the Layers palette on page 35

Quick Tip

Visibility
When working with multi-layered images it can help to temporarily hide one or more layers to get a better view of what you are doing. Photoshop allows you to hide layers by clicking on the little eye to the left of the layer thumbnail.

LAYER MANIPULATION ESSENTIALS

Layers are mainly controlled via the Layers palette. The Layers palette allows you to change the stacking order of layers, alter their Opacity, temporarily hide them and change the way they interact with those below using special Blending Modes. The best way to learn is to experiment – it's a lot less complex than it looks.

The Layers palette shows the order of the layers. Any layer can be dragged to a new position in the stack (though the Background Layer must be unlocked first).

You can reduce the **Opacity** of each individual layer – making it gradually more transparent. Note that doing this won't actually change the pixels in the layer, just how they appear.

Layers can be transformed, rotated, distorted, resized and duplicated with a few clicks. You'll find most of the controls under the **Edit>Transform** menu.

Since each layer can be edited independently you can delete an area of one without affecting any of the other layers in the document.

Layers can be grouped together so they can be moved or transformed simultaneously. You can also merge two or more layers into one.

Photoshop offers a range of special **Blending Modes** – these change the way the layer interacts with those below it (see page 32).

LAYER BLENDING MODES

Layer Blending Modes allow you to control how the colours and tones in a layer interact with those below. They're split into five broad sections.

The **Darken** group, including Multiply and several Burn options (depending on which version of Photoshop you're using). Darker colours always win here; white areas in the top layer never appear in these modes.

The **Lighten** group, including Screen and several Dodge options. White always wins here, whereas black areas have no effect in any of these modes.

The **Overlay** group, including Soft and Hard Light. These modes darken or lighten the underlying layer based on how bright each pixel is. Can be unpredictable.

The **Difference** and **Exclusion** modes look at the colours of the pixels in each layer and subtract the darker one from the lighter one. Have a few, very specific uses.

The **Hue**, **Saturation** and **Lightness** group. These modes use one aspect of the upper layer (such as Hue) to replace those values in the underlying layer. Has some uses.

Blending Modes

Every version of Photoshop comes with at least one new Layer Blending Mode, and to be honest most users stay away from them unless they're looking for a fast special effect. Blending Modes change the way in which the colours of the layer mix with those in the layer(s) below. The best way to get a feel for what each does is to experiment. We'll be using Blending Modes later for some special effects and advanced correction techniques, and as a quick and easy way to add some impact to an image by blending two copies of itself together (see pages 43 and 116).

LAYER STYLES

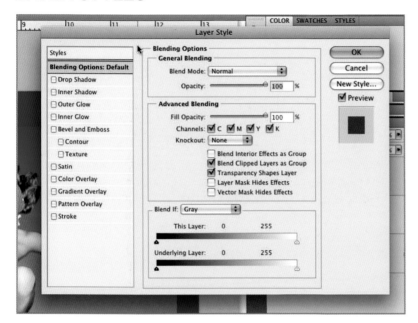

▲ Here is the Layer Styles panel for the Drop Shadow effect. There are options for the Size, Position and Opacity of the shadow and you can preview the changes as you make them.

Layer Styles are special effects that are applied to an entire layer in a non-destructive manner (in other words you can change or remove the style at any time). The Layer Styles dialog is invoked by double-clicking on a layer's thumbnail or by choosing one of the effects from the small pop-up menu at the bottom of the Layers palette. As the screenshot above shows, it's packed with a wealth of effects (each with its own set of

options) as well as some custom Blending Options for the layer in general (see page 34).

The effects themselves include drop shadows, lighting effects and overlays. You can combine any number of these effects and save the new style for future use. Although many of the effects are too graphic for use in photo editing, there are some that are invaluable when creating photo-montages or collages.

▲ Many of the effects – such as Drop Shadow – only work on layers with some transparent areas. You cannot apply a Layer Style to the locked Background Layer of a single, flat image – you need to promote it to an editable layer first, by double-clicking on it in the Layers palette.

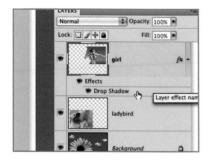

Layer Styles appear in the **Layers** palette. From here they can be hidden or deleted. Double-click on an effect to edit its settings.

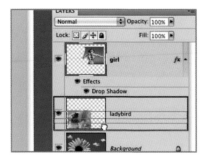

Effects can be copied from one layer to another or – as I'm doing here – dragged from one layer to a different one.

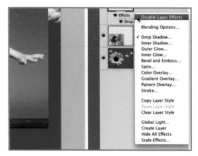

Right-click on the Layer Style in the Layers palette for a sub-menu of options for any effects you have applied, and for some global settings.

LAYER BLENDING OPTIONS

▲ The sliders in the Blending Options dialog box let you control exactly how the pixels in each layer blend based on their brightness.

If you move the right-hand arrows on the **This Layer** slider slightly to the left you will immediately see all the very lightest pixels disappear from the layer – position it correctly and the white background will be gone.

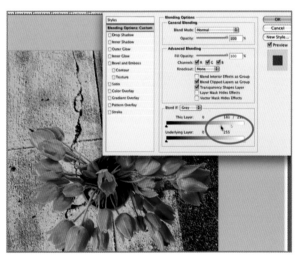

◄ Using the Alt (⌥) key you can split the slider to create a range of partially blended pixels, rather than a harsh cut-off point.

Moving the left-hand sliders to the right gradually hides shadow pixels. This is very useful for removing black backgrounds from a layer.

Blending Options

We've already seen the various ways two layers can interact using the Opacity and Blending Mode controls. Hidden in the Layer Styles dialog is another powerful tool – Blending Options. From here you can define how the layer blends with those below. The sliders in the Blending Options dialog box let you control which pixels from the active layer and which pixels from the underlying layers appear in the final image.

For example, you can drop dark pixels out of the active layer or force bright pixels from the underlying layer(s) to show through. This can be very useful for quick montage in situations like the one above, where the white background of the upper layer needs to be removed. Blended pixels are those that

THE LAYERS PALETTE

Although it's grown a few new features over the years the basic structure of the Layers palette hasn't changed a lot in the last few versions. Things can get pretty cluttered if you're working on a complex multi-layered document - this breakdown should help you make sense of things.

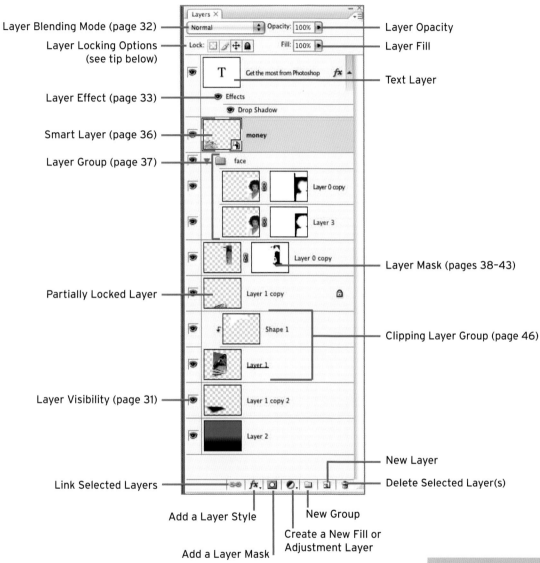

Layer Blending Mode (page 32) — Layer Opacity

Layer Locking Options (see tip below) — Layer Fill

Text Layer

Layer Effect (page 33) —

Smart Layer (page 36) —

Layer Group (page 37) —

Layer Mask (pages 38–43)

Partially Locked Layer —

Clipping Layer Group (page 46)

Layer Visibility (page 31) —

New Layer

Link Selected Layers — Delete Selected Layer(s)

Add a Layer Style

New Group

Create a New Fill or Adjustment Layer

Add a Layer Mask

will appear, unblended are those that won't. You can also define a range of partially blended pixels to produce a smooth transition between blended and unblended areas. Simply hold down the Alt (⌥) key as you drag to split the slider and define a range. Using this method, shots of lightning, the moon or even clouds can be overlaid on to other scenes in seconds by carefully controlling the tones that are blended and those that are hidden. A further example of this technique can be found on page 132.

Quick Tip

Layer Locking Options
Photoshop allows you to lock the transparent pixels, image pixels, and layer position independently (or you can lock everything). Locking transparent pixels allows you to paint on to a cut-out layer without going over the edge.

LAYER MENUS

The Layers palette has everything you need for most tasks, but there's plenty more in the Layer menu - and the Layer palette's own flyout menu.

The main Layer menu (this example is from Photoshop CS4, but the important stuff is the same in all versions). Again, most of the menu items duplicate the functions found on the Layers palette (or the Options bar), though it's useful to have them all in one place.

Click on the small black arrow at the top right corner and you'll see the Layers palette flyout menu. Many of the menu items are duplicated in the main Layer menu, or in the buttons/menus at the bottom of the Layers palette.

Layer Keyboard Shortcuts

New Empty Layer	Group Layers	Move Layer Up
Ctrl ⇧ – N / ⌘ ⇧	Ctrl – G / ⌘	Ctrl –] / ⌘
New Layer via Copy	**New Layer via Cut**	**Move Layer Down**
Ctrl – J / ⌘	Ctrl ⇧ – J / ⌘ ⇧	Ctrl – [/ ⌘

Layer Tips

■ The **Auto Layer Select** option is often more bane than boon with multi-layered documents. To temporarily activate it (so the layer under the cursor is automatically selected when you click) hold down the Ctrl (⌘) key while using the Move tool.

■ If you're doing a lot of layer transformations (such as when producing a complex montage) check the **Show Transform Controls** in the Move tool's Option bar and every layer you select will come complete with handles for stretching, distorting and rotating, without the need for menus.

Smart Layers (CS2+)

Photoshop CS2 saw the introduction of Smart Objects, and although some of the features will only be of interest to graphic designers, there are a couple of aspects that can be very useful in everyday photo manipulation - most specifically in photo-montage. When you convert a pixel-based layer into a Smart Object, Photoshop remembers all the original data in that layer, so you can transform it as many times as you want without loss (normally when you scale a layer down, for example, you lose information that doesn't return when you scale it back up again). You can also create multiple copies of a Smart Object and have

them all update if you change the original (though you can still apply Layer Styles - page 33 - or use Adjustment Layers - page 44 - on the individual copies).

Finally - and most usefully for everyday users - there are Smart Filters. Normally, if you apply a filter effect, such as blurring, to a layer the effect is basically irreversible (aside from choosing Undo). A Smart Filter acts a little like an Adjustment Layer, with the filter effect remaining separate from the layer itself. This means you can go back and remove the effect, change the strength of it, or mask the filter effect so it only affects part of the layer. This makes life easier and removes the need for backup copies of layers.

ORGANIZING LAYERS

Once you start working with multiple layers things can get a little complicated to say the least. Fortunately, Photoshop offers several ways to tame your Layers palette and organize your work.

Making life easier: once you've started to get more than a few layers in an image it can be difficult – if not impossible – to identify each element in your file from the Layers palette, especially if the sheer number forces you to use small thumbnails. To make things easier get into the habit of giving layers a proper name when they are first created or imported.

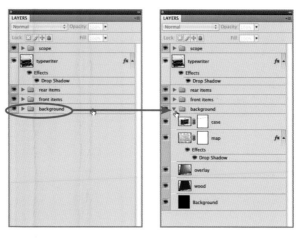

As well as linking layers (so they move and transform together) Photoshop allows you to group layers together into **Layer Sets** (versions 7.0 and CS) or **Layer Groups** (version CS2 and above). A Layer Group acts like a folder (and looks like one in the Layer palette). Options for Layer Groups include colour coding and the ability to choose a Blending Mode and Opacity for the entire group of layers.

Once organized into groups this highly complex montage becomes far easier to manage. The individual layers inside each group are still accessible and can be edited independently, or you can treat the entire group as one. This versatility means that Layer Groups don't just simplify the Layers palette – they simplify the entire process of managing multi-layered documents.

PHOTOSHOP BASICS: LAYER MASKS

Layer Masks allow you to experiment with effects and montages without permanently changing a single pixel.

Transparent areas can be created in any unlocked layer simply by deleting pixels. The problem with this approach - permanently removing parts of a layer - is that any deleted pixels cannot be restored later in the processing of an image. This can be a serious problem if you discover at some point later that your original editing was less than perfect, at which point you are faced with a stark choice; live with the problem or start all over again.

This is exactly what Layer Masks are designed to overcome. We've already dipped a toe into the world of masks when we refined a selection using Quick Mask mode (see page 28), and the principle behind Layer Masks is exactly the same. Layer Masks are grayscale channels that hide or reveal areas of a layer. Visually the result is exactly the same, but since you're only hiding, rather than deleting, pixels you can bring them back at any time.

The principle behind Layer Masks is simple; the opaque areas of the mask hide parts of the layer. The mask itself can be edited independently of the layer.

Layer | Layer Mask | Effect of Layer Mask | Backgroun Layer

DESTRUCTIVE EDITING

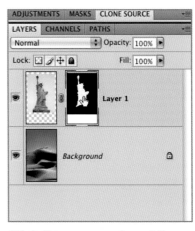

If you select an area of a layer and press Delete you can easily create a transparent area on a layer – and see through to the layers below.

Carrying this idea on, here I've used the Magic Wand to gradually select and delete the entire background from the upper layer.

Closer inspection reveals that I went a bit too far, deleting part of the layer I wanted to keep. No going back now, I just have to start again.

By using Layer Masks (and similar features such as Adjustment Layers and Smart Filters) you avoid burning your bridges, digitally speaking, and only commit to any changes you make to the pixels in your original image when you absolutely have to. This idea – commonly referred to as non-destructive editing – is key to efficient Photoshop workflow; not only can it save you hours of work if you make a mistake; it positively encourages experimentation, which is at the core of successful photo editing.

How Masks Work

Technically speaking a Layer Mask is an 8-bit grayscale channel associated with a specific layer that is used to define the Opacity (or transparency if you prefer) of every single pixel in the layer (since every pixel in the layer has a corresponding pixel in the mask).

Mask pixels can have any value from 0 (black) to 255 (white); black pixels in the mask make completely transparent layer pixels, white pixels in the mask make completely opaque pixels. Mask areas that are any other value (in other words any shade of grey) produce semi-transparent areas in the layer.

Since a Layer Mask – like the Quick Mask we looked at on pages 27-28 – is a grayscale image, you can use Photoshop's full range of tools, effects and filters directly on the mask. Using a black to white gradient on a mask, for example, is a very quick way to get one layer to gently blend into another.

This is the same example as at the top of the page, only this time the background of the upper layer has been masked, not deleted. This is non-destructive editing.

GETTING STARTED WITH LAYER MASKS

The easiest way to get your head round how Layer Masks work is to dive straight in and start creating and editing them. Here's how.

Start with a simple document containing two layers (see page 37 for quick tips on combining several different pictures into multi-layered Photoshop files).

Make sure the upper layer is selected and from the **Layer** menu choose **Layer Mask>Reveal All**. As with most things in Photoshop, this is just one of several ways to add a mask.

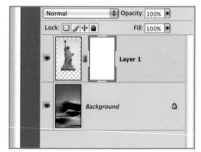

If you look at the **Layers** palette you'll see that there's a new thumbnail next to the layer thumbnail. It shows the mask, which is currently all-white, so no part of the layer is being hidden.

If you click on the **Layer Mask** thumbnail you can edit it directly. Here, I'm using a large brush with black 'paint' (the Foreground Color) to make parts of the layer transparent.

Here, I've used a white to black gradient from the top to bottom of the mask. As the mask gets darker it gradually hides more of the layer.

Masks are hugely important in montage. Here, I've used the mask to make all the background areas of the upper layer transparent.

So, here's what you need to remember. White paint on the mask makes layer pixels opaque. Use white to reveal more of the layer.

Using black paint on the mask, on the other hand, makes layer pixels transparent; use black paint to hide areas of the layer.

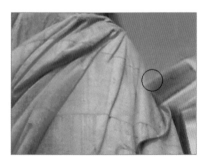

Using a larger soft-edged brush creates a smooth transition between opaque and transparent areas. Use grey paint to produce semi-transparent areas on the layer.

The Advantage of Masks

All the examples we've looked at so far involve basic photo-montage – combining two or more shots into a single composition. Masks are invaluable in such situations as they allow a flexibility that simply cutting out elements (i.e. deleting any areas not wanted) doesn't offer, but as you'll discover working through this book, masks make their way into pretty much every aspect of Photoshop technique.

A good example is selective adjustments, where you apply a tonal change to part, but not all of an image – such as when you want to darken a sky without changing the foreground brightness.

The simple approach is to select the sky area before changing the brightness, but this is a destructive edit; the pixels are changed permanently, and there's no going back later if you change your mind. A far better approach is to make a copy layer and change that. You can then use a Layer Mask to define which areas of the new, edited layer are visible and which aren't. The advantage of an approach like this is that you're not stuck with the selection made in the first step (the mask can always be edited). Using masks also allows you to go back and change the effect itself – in the example mentioned you could decide later that you hadn't darkened the sky enough – or had gone too far. If you didn't permanently alter the original pixels it's a simple matter to change the effect without having to start from scratch.

We'll be using Layer Masks extensively in the step-by-step projects later on (see page 72 onwards) so it's worth spending time playing around with them and trying out some of the simple examples in this section yourself.

Mask Tips

Disabling Masks
Shift-click on a mask's thumbnail to temporarily disable it.

Mask Menu
Right-click on the mask's thumbnail for a useful sub-menu of options.

Unlink
Masks are normally linked to their layer (so they move together), but you can unlink the mask and move it on its own.

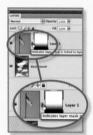

MASKS FROM SELECTIONS

With an active selection click on the **Add Layer Mask** icon at the bottom of the Layers palette (or choose the option from the Layer menu). By default the mask hides everything you had selected.

Hold down the Alt (⌥) key when you click the Add Layer Mask icon (or choose Layer>Layer Mask>Reveal Selection) to do the opposite; hide everything outside the selection.

You can turn a mask into a selection too, via the Select>Load Selection... menu. Or you can hold down the Ctrl (⌘) key and click on the Layer Mask thumbnail.

LAYER MASKS FOR SELECTIVE EFFECTS

Masks aren't only for combining several images into one; they're incredibly powerful for selective creative effects without permanently altering pixels.

By duplicating the Background Layer of an image you can apply filters, blurring, colour changes and so on to one of the layers and add a mask to restrict the effects to specific areas.

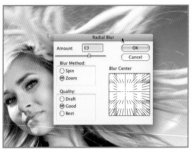

Here, I'm applying a heavy **Radial Blur** (**Filter>Blur>Radial Blur**) to the upper (duplicated) layer, but it could be any filter or effect from a simple colour tweak to a major distortion like this.

The effect is impressive, but it completely obliterates the model's face, which really defeats the point of the image.

By adding a **Layer Mask** you can use a large, soft brush to hide the area of the blurred layer around the face.

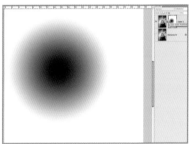

Here's the mask – as you can see it's a very simple thing. The black areas will mask the layer.

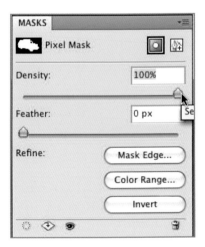

And here's the result of the mask on the upper layer (I've temporarily hidden the original Background Layer which is, of course, unchanged).

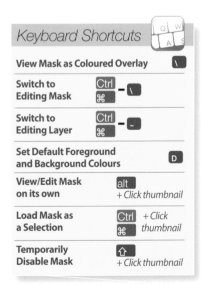

Keyboard Shortcuts	
View Mask as Coloured Overlay	\
Switch to Editing Mask	Ctrl ⌘ – \
Switch to Editing Layer	Ctrl ⌘ – ~
Set Default Foreground and Background Colours	D
View/Edit Mask on its own	alt + Click thumbnail
Load Mask as a Selection	Ctrl ⌘ + Click thumbnail
Temporarily Disable Mask	⇧ + Click thumbnail

Refining Masks

The Layer Masking tools have remained fairly unchanged for many years, but CS4 did see the introduction of a useful new palette for fine-tuning mask edges (allowing you to add feathering and to reduce the Density of the mask). It's also worth noting that CS3's Refine Edge tool (see page 26) can be used on a mask. If you're using earlier versions fear not, there are plenty of tricks later in the book for fine-tuning masks.

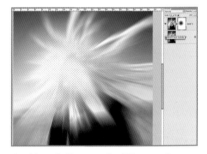

▲ **Photoshop CS4's new Masks palette.**

TRY THIS: LAYER SANDWICHES

One quick way to transform an image is to use a duplicate of the Background Layer with one of Photoshop's many Blending Modes. With a Layer Mask you can also restrict the effect to a specific area of the frame.

Start by duplicating the Background Layer (the quickest way to do this is to press Ctrl-J (⌘-J).

Experiment with the different Layer Blending Modes (see page 32). The Darken group (including **Color Burn** used here) increase contrast overall.

Not surprisingly, the Lighten group of Blending Modes (this is **Color Dodge**) lighten the image and produce very bright, 'contrasty' results.

The **Hard Mix** mode produces an almost comic-like result with grossly exaggerated colours.

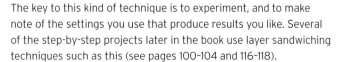

Here, the **Vivid Light** mode was used with a Layer Mask around the face, allowing control over where the effect appears for a subtler result.

The key to this kind of technique is to experiment, and to make note of the settings you use that produce results you like. Several of the step-by-step projects later in the book use layer sandwiching techniques such as this (see pages 100–104 and 116–118).

PHOTOSHOP BASICS:
ADJUSTMENT LAYERS

One of Photoshop's most useful tools gives you the ability to adjust colour and contrast in any part of the frame without permanently changing anything.

On page 43 we looked at using duplicate layers to apply tonal changes to images without permanently altering the original pixels, something we'll cover in more depth in Chapter Five (see pages 71–92). However Photoshop offers a considerably more elegant way to apply tonal changes selectively to areas of an image, using an Adjustment Layer. Adjustment Layers are special layers containing a tonal adjustment (such as Levels, Curves or Hue/Saturation) and

a Layer Mask, which defines which parts of the image are affected.

The advantage of an Adjustment Layer is twofold; you can go back at any time and change the setting used (or remove it entirely) and you can alter the areas affected by simply painting on to the Adjustment Layer's mask.

Depending on the version of Photoshop you're using you can create an Adjustment Layer using any of the following adjustments: Levels, Curves, Color Balance,

Brightness/Contrast, Black & White, Hue/Saturation, Selective Color, Channel Mixer, Gradient Map, Photo Filter, Exposure, Invert, Threshold and Posterize. All Adjustment Layers are created with a mask by default (though you can actually delete the mask if you don't need it), and the mask is edited and manipulated in exactly the same way as a standard Layer Mask (see page 40). Layer Masks can also be placed anywhere in the layer stack, and they will only affect layers below.

Using an Adjustment Layer allows you to experiment with colour and tonal changes without ever committing to changing the underlying pixels. Here, a Hue/Saturation Adjustment Layer has been used to alter the Hue dramatically; a mask restricts the changes to a specific area of the image.

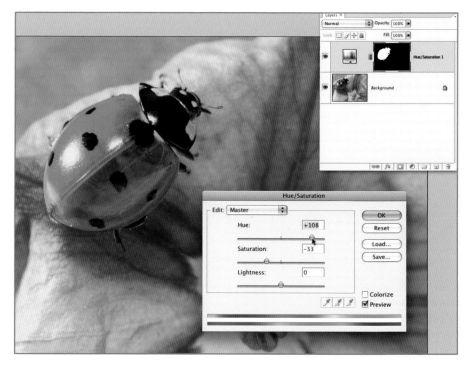

ADJUSTMENT LAYER ESSENTIALS

**As usual, the easiest way to understand Adjustment Layers is to see them in action.
So let's walk through their creation and see what they are capable of:**

Adjustment Layers are created using the Layer>New Adjustment Layer... menu; simply pick the adjustment you want to apply (the choices will vary slightly depending on which version of Photoshop you're using).

For this example I've chosen a simple **Levels** adjustment for altering the brightness and contrast of the image. By default the new layer is called Levels 1. Just click OK to create it.

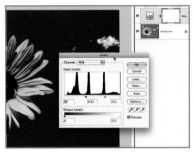

Unless you're using CS4 the dialog box for the chosen adjustment will appear immediately (CS4 uses a separate **Adjustments** palette, but the process is identical). Here, I've used Levels to darken the image.

By default the Adjustment Layer affects the entire image; its mask is completely white. Here, I'm using a large brush to paint with black on to the mask, which is hiding (masking) the effect.

Here, I've used a large soft-edged brush to mask the area around the flower. The flower is now as bright as it was when I started; the rest of the frame is darker thanks to the effect of the Adjustment Layer.

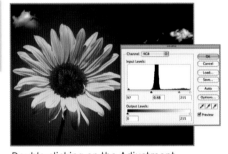

Double-clicking on the Adjustment Layer's icon brings back the dialog for the adjustment itself, allowing you to change the Levels setting; here, I've made it really dark.

Like a standard Layer Mask, an Adjustment Layer's mask can be created directly from a live selection. This is a Hue/Saturation layer.

And just like any other Layer Mask you can fine-tune the Adjustment Layer, using a small brush and black to hide the effect, white to reveal it.

This allows you to apply the effect seamlessly and to go back at any point and edit the mask – or change the strength of the adjustment.

The sheer versatility offered by Adjustment Layers means they have almost limitless uses – for example I often use a high-contrast Levels Adjustment Layer to make it easier to find edges when making complex selections – the Adjustment Layer is thrown away once I've done with it. In fact, for anything but the simplest quick tweaks you should get into the habit of using Adjustment Layers for all tonal and colour changes.

The reason comes back to the old 'destructive versus non-destructive' editing argument. Even a minor tonal adjustment (such as slightly brightening an image using Levels) results in the loss of some of the original information in the file you're working on, and if it's a long, complex multi-step project these small losses can start to add up. There's nothing worse than looking at two hour's work and thinking, 'Hmm, maybe I shouldn't

have increased the contrast quite so much back at the start.' Even with a simple single-step tonal change you can do a lot more experimenting if you use an Adjustment Layer – and you'll never need to use the Undo command ever again.

Finally, it's worth noting that Photoshop CS4 has a very slightly different way of working with Adjustment Layers thanks to its new Adjustments palette, which replaces the standard dialog box for the adjustment being applied and allows one-click creation of Adjustment Layers. In every other respect CS4's Adjustment Layers are the same as in every other version of the software.

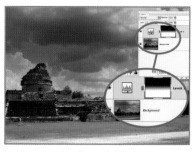

▲ One practical use for Adjustment Layers is to lighten one part of the frame (the lower part of this shot) while leaving the rest (the sky) untouched. A soft gradient from top to bottom on the mask produces a gentle transition between the adjusted and unadjusted areas of the frame.

Photoshop CS4's new Adjustments palette offers one-click creation of Adjustment Layers as well as a wide range of useful Presets for each of the adjustments on offer.

CLIPPING LAYERS

When using Adjustment Layers in a montage, you often want the adjustment to only affect one element. Fortunately Photoshop offers an easy way to do this – and you don't need a selection or a mask.

Make sure you click on the layer you want to work on first. When you create the new Adjustment Layer check the **Use Previous Layer to Create Clipping Mask** option.

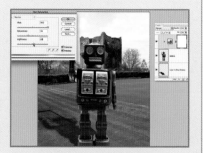

The Adjustment Layer now uses the transparency of the layer it uses as a Clipping Mask. This means that even if you change the clipping layer the adjustment will always match perfectly.

CHAPTER FOUR

KEY PHOTO CORRECTIONS

Whether you're shooting with the latest digital SLR or scanning old photos from a shoebox, the chances are that your images will need a little help in order to really shine. This chapter looks at some of Photoshop's essential tools for correcting, enhancing and, if necessary, completely transforming your photographs.

When first faced with the seemingly endless array of tools and options for tonal corrections on offer, it's hardly surprising that many Photoshop novices end up tearing their hair out trying to work out which they should be using.

Yet the truth is, that like so many things in an application this big and this mature, most of Photoshop's tonal controls simply offer different ways to achieve the same result. And they mostly boil down to three things: brightness, contrast and colour. This chapter will cover the most frequently used controls for altering these three variables, as well as looking at the other basic tweaks commonly applied to most digital images; sharpening, straightening

and cropping. In Chapter Five we'll look in a little more detail at some specific techniques for putting the tools covered here to use for sorting out the kinds of problems often found in digital photos.

It's important to remember that for the most part there is no right or wrong tool to use for adjusting image contrast, exposure or colour, though some are better suited to certain situations than others. I personally use Levels (see page 48) far more often than I use Curves (see page 54), even though Curves offers a finer level of control, because Levels is fast and easy. The important thing is to understand what the various tools do, and to find a workflow that suits the way you want to do things.

KEY PHOTO CORRECTIONS:
LEVELS AND HISTOGRAMS

We'll dive straight in with Levels; a powerful all-in-one solution for fixing brightness, colour and contrast in a single, easy-to-comprehend dialog.

Given that Photoshop offers a very simple tool for adjusting brightness and contrast – the aptly named Brightness/Contrast control – it might seem a little odd to start with Levels (both can be found under the Image>Adjustments menu). But I do so with good reason: Levels is a powerful tool for correcting brightness, contrast and colour balance in as little as three clicks. Not only that, Levels is also relatively simple to use and easy to understand exactly what is going on.

Because Levels lets you work directly with the Histogram (see below) I've always found it to be one of the more intuitive of Photoshop's advanced controls, and it's an ideal starting point for anyone who wants to learn how to fix problems intelligently, rather than randomly moving sliders until the picture looks OK.

The Histogram (which you can also see if you choose Window>Info or press F8) is a graph that shows the distribution

LEVELS AND HISTOGRAMS

Before you can start to use Photoshop's more advanced tonal controls you need to learn how to read a Histogram – and there's one right at the heart of the Levels dialog.

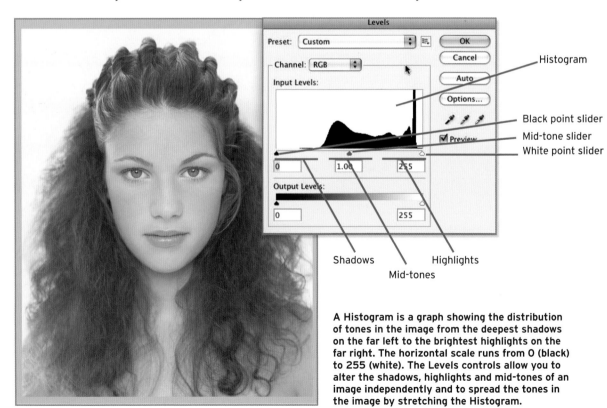

A Histogram is a graph showing the distribution of tones in the image from the deepest shadows on the far left to the brightest highlights on the far right. The horizontal scale runs from 0 (black) to 255 (white). The Levels controls allow you to alter the shadows, highlights and mid-tones of an image independently and to spread the tones in the image by stretching the Histogram.

of image brightnesses from (left to right) black to white. The Levels controls consist of three sliders that allow you to reposition the white, black and mid-grey points.

Learning to read Histograms is essential to ensuring you get the exposure right in the first place, or that you take the right steps to rectify problems. You may already be familiar with Histograms from your digital camera, but if not the examples on the right and over the page should help you out.

THE LEVELS SLIDERS

The black slider under the Histogram represents the black point of the image (0 on the scale 0-255). Try sliding it to the right and see what happens to the preview image. You will see the shadow areas of the picture get darker. To correct this pale image you need to move the slider to the point where the graph tails off to zero. Moving the white point slider to the left will make all the highlights brighter.

Now try moving the middle (grey) slider from left to right. This adjustment (called a Gamma adjustment) lightens or darkens mid-tones without overly affecting the shadows or highlights. What you're actually doing is defining where on the 0-255 scale (black to white) the mid-grey point will sit.

INTERPRETING HISTOGRAMS

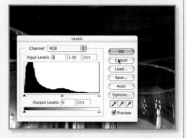

Low Key: Although the majority of pixels in this image are in the darkest quarter of the graph, there is still a spread of tones right over to the brightest value (255).

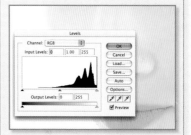

High Key: In this case the majority of pixels are at the extreme highlight end, but they are not bunched up and don't seem to go off the end of the scale, so this image is light, but not overexposed.

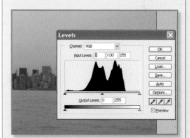

Low Contrast: Typical of many digital cameras – especially older models – and hazy weather, this image shows that the camera has not used the entire range of available tones (from pure black to pure white) to represent the brightness levels in the scene. There is little or no dark shadow and no pixels at all in the brightest quarter or so of the range. The image is not, however, under or overexposed, and can be easily fixed using Levels.

AUTOMATIC ADJUSTMENTS

Photoshop offers some automatic Levels adjustments that are worth a try, though the results can be hit and miss. These can be accessed from the Adjustments menu or you can try them from within the Levels dialog itself, by clicking the Options button.

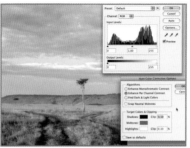

The first option (**Enhance Mono-chromatic Contrast**) is the same as choosing **Auto Contrast** from the menu. It fixes the black and white points for better contrast.

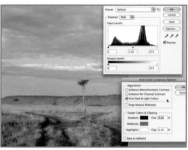

Enhance Per Channel Contrast automatically sets the black and white points for each channel separately, so attempts to fix colour casts. This is the same as choosing **Auto Levels**.

Finally there's **Find Dark and Light Colors** (the same as **Auto Color**), which analyses the image itself (not just the Histograms) for a better result (colour and contrast).

INTERPRETING HISTOGRAMS

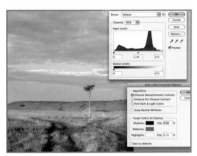

Overexposed: In an overexposed image the Histogram appears bunched up on the right-hand side, while there are no pixels at all in the shadow range. Most levels are off the scale and appear as pure white.

Underexposed: Again, the Histogram is bunched up, this time at the left side, with virtually nothing in the highlight area. Most pixels are off the scale on the other side, and appear as pure black.

So what's actually happening when you use Levels to make adjustments?

As you move the black and white point sliders you are redefining the black and white points of the image. The grey slider changes the graph relating input (the picture before you started) to output from a straight line to a curve. Look at the example below. The white slider has been moved from the 255 position to 209. This means all pixels with a brightness value of between 209 and 255 will now be remapped to 255 (pure white), and the Histogram stretched to fill the gap.

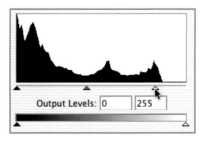

This is why you move the white slider to the point on the Histogram where the graph tails away to zero - this is the brightest part of your image, and you are defining this as the white point. In the example below there are no pixels at all in the 218-255 range. By moving the slider you are saying 'make 217 the new 255 and remap the other tones to fit'.

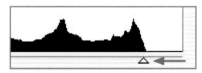

The same applies for images where the darkest tones are not black - use the black slider to redefine the black point, as below.

USING THE EYEDROPPERS

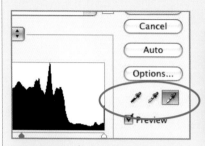  

In the bottom right-hand corner of the Levels dialog you'll find three **Eyedropper** tools – black, grey and white. You can use these to quickly define the white and black points (and colour balance) of your image.

To set a new white point select the white Eyedropper and choose a point in your image you want to be white. This should be the brightest part of the picture that still contains information.

Click the mouse button and you'll see the entire image has been remapped to the white point you selected. Now you can do exactly the same for the black point.

With the black Eyedropper, click on the darkest point of your image. You have now set the black point.

You'll notice the Levels Eyedroppers don't only affect brightness, they also affect colour. The middle Eyedropper – the grey one – can be used to define neutral grey, with the rest of the image remapped to fit.

You can keep re-clicking until you find the right point – the on-screen preview will allow you to visually assess the result of each point you sample.

Highlight or Not?

When using Levels, it is important that you set the white point to the brightest printable highlight, which is not necessarily the brightest point in the image. This is due to so-called 'specular highlights', caused by glare or overexposure. The same is true to a certain extent for some images with some totally black pixels, which received no exposure at all. Because of this we tend to set the white point slightly in from where the Histogram first shows values in the highlight region (shown below with the red arrow).

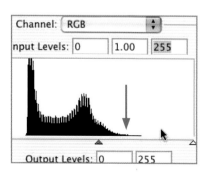

Quick Tip

Threshold Mode
Hold down the Alt (⌥) key as you drag the black or white sliders and the preview will show which pixels will be remapped to pure black or white.

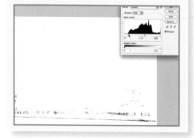

USING LEVELS ON COLOUR CHANNELS

Like most of Photoshop's tonal correction tools, Levels can be used on the individual colour channels of an image independently.

■ Try to get into the habit of using a **Levels Adjustment Layer** (see page 44) – this not only allows you to change the setting at any point in the future, it also allows you to use a mask to apply the effect selectively to a certain part of the frame.

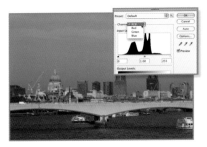

If you click on the **Channel** menu in the Levels dialog you'll see that you can choose to adjust the contrast of a single colour channel. We're going to use this feature to fix the colour and contrast of this shot at the same time but you can also use it for subtler colour tweaks.

Let's start with the **Red** channel. All I'm doing here is placing the white and black points in the same way I would if I were fixing the contrast of an image in RGB mode; moving the sliders so they're just beyond the point where the levels on the Histogram drop to zero.

■ Although there is no Auto Levels Adjustment Layer in Photoshop, you can create one using a normal Levels Adjustment Layer and clicking on **Auto** in the Levels dialog.

■ If you want to make Levels or Auto Levels adjustments to an entire image, based only on the tones in a small section of the frame you can, using an Adjustment Layer:
(i) Draw a selection around the area of the image you want the changes to be based on (for example the face of a studio portrait).

(ii) With the selection active, create a new Levels Adjustment Layer. You will see the normal Levels dialog, with the Histogram based only on the selection you just made.

(iii) Make the adjustments necessary to correct the area you are interested in.

(iv) Click on OK. Now delete the Layer Mask. You will see that the entire image has now been affected by the Levels adjustments.

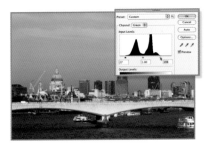

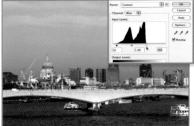

Here, I've switched to the **Green** channel and am doing the same thing.

And finally the **Blue** channel. I can now go back and fine-tune the settings for each of the three channels to get the exact colour balance I want.

Choose Histogram from the View menu and All Channels View from the Histogram palette's flyout options menu and you can quickly see which of the colour channels need fixing.

SHADOW/HIGHLIGHT ADJUSTMENT

Photoshop CS saw the introduction of a powerful and useful new tool for pulling detail out of shadow areas with almost incredible ease. The Shadow/Highlight tool (**Image> Adjustments>Shadow/Highlight...**) has a very simple interface but there's some pretty complex work going on behind the scenes, and – if used carefully – you can get results in seconds that would take a lot longer using Levels.

Technically, the Shadow/ Highlight tool uses a process called 'contrast masking' to increase brightness only in the darkest areas of the image frame. You can also use it to tone down strong highlights and restore the balance in your images. Let's take a look at it in action.

Here's the starting image with the **Shadows** and **Highlights** sliders both set to zero (no effect). This shot has been slightly underexposed because the bright sky has fooled the camera's metering system.

Moving the Shadows slider magically brightens the darkest areas without really affecting the highlights at all. The default setting is 50%, but you may find this to be a bit extreme, so experiment.

Moving the Highlights slider gradually darkens the lighter parts of the image. You want to use this one sparingly as the result can start to look rather unnatural.

If you're feeling adventurous, click on **Show More Options** – from here you can define how broad the highlight and shadow ranges are (**Tonal Width**) and how harsh the cut-off around the affected areas is (**Radius**). There are also sliders for **Color Correction** and **Midtone Contrast** to play with.

KEY CORRECTIONS:
CURVES

Getting to grips with Curves is vital if you want total control over the tonality of your images.

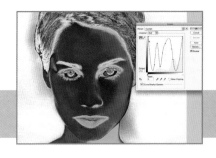

Curves (**Image>Adjustments> Curves**) is not the most user-friendly tool in the digital darkroom. But, with a little practice, you can do things with Curves that are all but impossible with any other tool. This is especially true when dealing with awkward pictures – those with exposure or contrast problems. By adding several points to the curve it is possible to fine-tune the tones within the image in a way not possible using Brightness/Contrast or Levels (which can't be used to reduce contrast, for example).

For most serious users, Curves is the first stop when adjusting contrast. The best way to learn how the Curves tool can change your photos is to experiment, so have a look at the examples on the right and then try them out on your own images.

UNDERSTANDING CURVES

The curve represents the relationship between Input (the horizontal axis) and Output (the vertical axis) brightness values. So, the horizontal axis shows all the tones in your image left to right from the darkest (0, absolute black) to the brightest (255, white). The vertical axis represents the tones after the curves have been applied. When you open the Curves dialog the graph is a straight line at 45-degrees – the Input and Output values are identical. By changing the shape – or angle – of the curve you remap the Input values to new (Output) values. To move the curve, simply click on one of the end points and drag it, or click on the line itself and drag to add a new point and make the line curved.

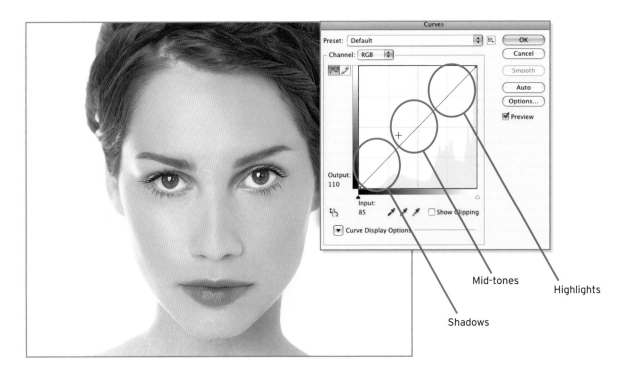

Mid-tones

Highlights

Shadows

BASIC CURVES ADJUSTMENTS

Let's start with the most basic Curves adjustments and how they affect the image. The important thing to remember here is that a steeper angle increases contrast, while a shallower angle reduces contrast. Where the curve drops below the 45-degree line tones get darker, where it rises above it tones get lighter. The red lines on these illustrations show how mid-grey in the original image is lightened or darkened by the changes made.

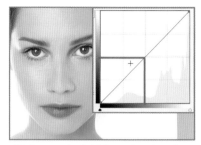

45-degree straight line – Input and Output values are the same.

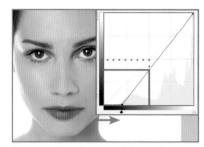

Increased contrast and darkening of all tones.

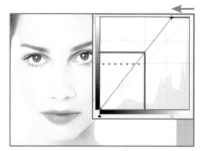

Increased contrast and lightening of all tones.

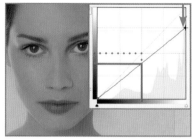

Reduced contrast and darkening of all tones.

Reduced contrast and lightening of all tones.

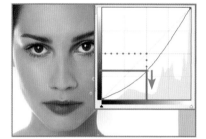

Mid-tones darkened – shadows and highlights unaffected.

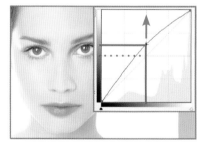

Mid-tones lightened – shadows and highlights unaffected.

Dragging the highlight area up and the shadow area down produces this classic 'S' shape which increases contrast without losing too much information in the mid-tones. This can be further refined to get exactly the tonal range you are looking for.

CURVES AND COLOUR

As with most tools you can adjust the curves for each colour channel independently. To manipulate the curves for one of the Red, Green and Blue channels you need to select it from the Channel drop-down menu.

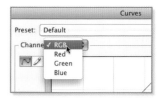

Start with the **Red** channel. Moving the curve upwards increases the amount of red in the image.

Pulling the Red channel curve down makes the image bluer (technically speaking, more cyan).

Now switch to the **Blue** channel. Not surprisingly, pushing the blue curve upwards makes the image bluer.

Pulling the blue curve downwards makes the image yellower (useful for adding warmth to evening shots).

No prizes for guessing what happens if you push the **Green** channel curve upwards; the picture gets greener.

The opposite of green is magenta, so pulling the green curve downwards adds an increasingly pink tinge.

Here, I've tweaked all three curves to make a much warmer evening glow effect. Note that the curves have not been moved that far – it's always best to start with a subtle effect as it's easy to go mad with Curves and end up with something totally psychedelic.

In the previous example, the only thing I did was to change the angle of the curve (it was still a straight line) – this is no different to using the **Color Balance** sliders (**Image>Adjustments>Color Balance**). Here, I've used Curves to produce a stronger result.

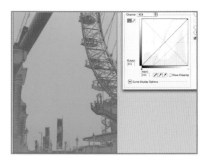

Here, I've gone for a deliberately graphic posterized effect, reversing the red curve completely and pushing the green contrast very hard. I've also removed pretty much all the blue from the scene. If you find an effect you like, hit **Save** to save it as a new Curves **Preset**.

ADJUSTING CONTRAST WITH CURVES

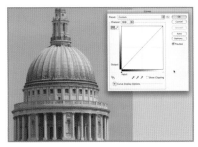

We'll start with this rather flat, haze-filled shot.

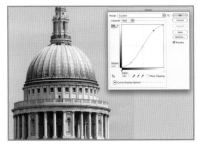

A simple, gentle 'S' curve increases contrast without changing mid-tones.

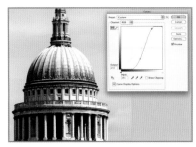

A steeper curve increases contrast further, but clipping occurs.

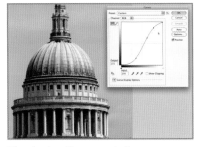

Fine-tuning the curve to increase contrast and protect the highlights.

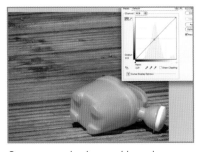

Curves can also be used to reduce contrast when necessary.

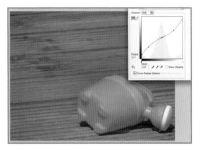

This inverted 'S' curve does the job perfectly.

FIXING SIMPLE COLOUR CASTS

This image is obviously way too green so I've selected the **Green** channel.

Dragging the green curve down fixes the colour cast in a couple of seconds.

It's worth mentioning at this point that Photoshop CS3 introduced a revamped Curves dialog with a couple of important new features. The first is the ability to display a Histogram behind the Curve, and the dialog now sports black and white point sliders (just like you'll find in Levels), which makes it faster and easier to increase contrast even if you're not that familiar with using Curves. The CS3 dialog is also larger and cleaner and offers some useful Presets (you can also save your own curves as Presets).

Curves Tips

■ Remember that when working on individual colour channels, dragging the curve UP increases the amount of that colour, DOWN reduces the amount.

■ Even the smallest changes in the curve can have a significant effect, so start with gentle changes.

■ Click on any anchor point on the curve and drag it off the graph to remove it.

■ Use a **Curves Adjustment Layer** (see page 44) so you can go back and change the settings later and mask the effect to apply it to a specific area of the frame.

■ The Curves dialog has an **Auto** button. Try this and look at the individual channel curves afterwards to see what has been done to get the result you see – you'll learn a lot.

ADVANCED CURVES TECHNIQUES

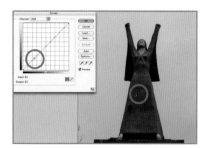

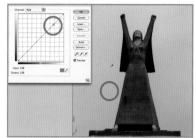

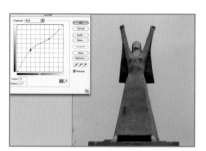

It can be very useful to know where on the curve a particular tone in the image lies. If you click in the image itself you'll see a small hollow circle appear on the curve. Here, I've clicked in the middle of the statue, and can see it lies around a quarter of the way in from the left.

Clicking and dragging around the sky area shows that it lies around a quarter of the way in from the right. I want to brighten the statue without completely burning out the blue sky, so armed with this information I can add an anchor point to protect these tones.

With the anchor in place I can now click and drag the curve upwards in the area I identified as being where most of the tones in the statue lie without really touching the sky tones. The result is to lighten the statue without burning out the sky.

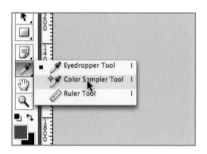

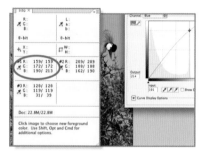

The **Color Sampler** tool is useful for checking the results of changes to the individual colour channels. You'll need the **Info** panel open too (press F8).

Click anywhere in the frame to add a Color Sampler - the RGB values for each is shown on the Info panel (they are numbered as you create them).

As you change the curve the Info panel updates to show before and after RGB values for each Color Sampler. We'll be using this on page 87 to fix problem colours.

By careful manipulation of the curve - and by using the Sampler and Eyedroppers to check which parts of the curve you need to adjust, it's possible to lift shadows without clipping even the brightest highlights.

STEP-BY-STEP: CONTRAST AND COLOUR TRANSFORMATION

We've had plenty of theory now, so let's take a walk through an example of how you can quickly transform a dull, flat and lifeless shot into something with a lot more contrast and a real sunset atmosphere in a few simple steps. This could be done without Curves, but no other tool offers such a wide range of controls over contrast and colour.

STEP 01

We'll start with this digital shot of the New York skyline from top of the Empire State Building. Unfortunately the weather conditions didn't do justice to the view.

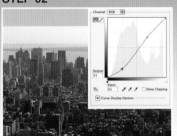

STEP 02

First to reduce the haze by increasing the contrast of the mid-tones and shadows. One anchor point protects the highlights, the other pulls down the darker part of the curve.

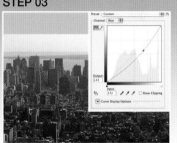

STEP 03

I want to remove the cool colour of the original shot so I'm going to need to start by selecting the **Blue** channel and pulling the curve down.

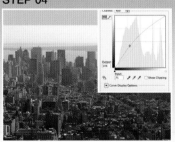

STEP 04

Next the reds. Working on the **Red** channel I'm lifting the curve. This is a creative process, not a colour fix, so I'm experimenting visually with how far I adjust each curve.

STEP 05

It was obvious during the last step that I'd need to pull a little green out of the mid-tones. This is a simple case of selecting the **Green** channel and dragging the curve down a touch.

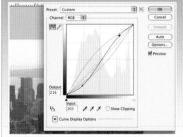

STEP 06

Going back to the **RGB** curves lets you look at what you've done. The result is the rescue of a shot that might otherwise have ended up in the trash.

KEY PHOTO CORRECTIONS:
HUE/SATURATION

Photoshop's Hue/Saturation adjustments offer an invaluable set of tools for boosting, toning down or shifting colours in an image.

Computers and digital cameras tend to store colour information as values of Red, Green and Blue (RGB). The same colour information can also be described using several other systems, of which Hue, Saturation and Lightness (HSL) is just one. HSL splits the colour into three variables using a colour wheel; Hue (the colour - the position on the colour wheel), Saturation (strength or purity of the colour) and Lightness. Photoshop's Hue/Saturation controls allow you to make subtle - or sweeping - changes to colour without affecting brightness or contrast.

HUE/SATURATION BASICS

The Image>Adjustments>Hue/Saturation menu is where you start. There are sliders for **Hue** (colour), **Saturation** (strength) and **Lightness**.

The **Saturation** slider controls the intensity of the colour (to be more specific it controls the amount of grey in the colour). Increasing Saturation makes colours more vivid.

Reducing the Saturation of an image moves it closer to grey, with less intense, less vivid colours. If you take the Saturation all the way to zero you end up with a grayscale image.

A colour's Hue can be defined as its position on a traditional colour wheel, and moving the **Hue** slider rotates all the colours on the wheel by a certain number of degrees.

As you move the slider you'll see every colour in the frame changes drastically (the two colour scales at the bottom of the HSL dialog box show the before and after tones). It's very rare to use the Hue slider on an entire image.

The **Lightness** slider isn't one you'll use that often. Increasing it moves every colour towards white, reducing it moves every colour towards black.

COLOUR SPECIFIC HUE/SATURATION ADJUSTMENTS

One of the most useful features of the HSL controls is the ability to restrict the effect of any changes to a particular group of colours.

This allows you to, for example, boost the blue of a sky or reduce the redness of a sunburnt face without actually having to make

a selection, thereby saving you some time. It's also a useful way to get rid of colour noise in high-ISO digital shots.

To edit a single group of colours pick one from the drop-down menu. You can also use the **Color Sampler** to pick colours directly from the image.

Here, we're working only on the **Reds** in the frame; a quick way to change the colour of this bright red London bus without changing all the other colours in the scene.

And here we're reducing the Saturation and Lightness of the **Blues** to turn a glorious summer sky into one that looks ominous and grey.

One of the most common uses for the Hue/Saturation controls is the Colorize option. This allows you to remove all the original colour from the shot and results in a toned mono image. This makes producing sepia images as easy as a couple of clicks.

Quick Tip

The **Hue/Saturation** controls offer a fast way to deal with red skin (such as in this holiday shot).

Choosing to edit the **Reds** you can reduce the Saturation and move the Hue slightly to the right (which makes them more yellow) and hey presto; tanned not burnt.

The following menu is shown at the top right:

Image
Mode   ▶
Adjustments   ▶   Levels...   ⌘L
Duplicate...   Auto Levels   ⇧⌘L
Apply Image...   Auto Contrast   ⌥⇧⌘L
Calculations...   Auto Color   ⇧⌘B
                             Curves...   ⌘M
Image Size...   ⌥⌘I   Color Balance...   ⌘B
Canvas Size...   ⌥⌘C   Brightness/Contrast...
Pixel Aspect Ratio   ▶
Rotate Canvas   ▶   Black & White...   ⌥⇧⌘B
Crop   Hue/Saturation...   ⌘U
Trim...   Desaturate   ⇧⌘U
Reveal All   Match Color...
                             Replace Color...
Variables   ▶   Selective Color...
Apply Data Set...   Channel Mixer...
                             Gradient Map...
Trap...   Photo Filter...
                             Shadow/Highlight...
                             Exposure...

                             Invert   ⌘I
                             Equalize
                             Threshold...
                             Posterize...

                             Variations...

KEY CORRECTIONS:
OTHER ADJUSTMENTS

We've only really scratched the surface of Photoshop's Adjustment tools ... so here's a few more.

Over the past dozen or so pages we've looked in detail at the key image adjustment tools that every serious Photoshop user needs to master, and those we'll be using most often in the step-by-step projects to follow. But no matter which version of Photoshop you're using, you'll have noticed that there's a lot more on offer under the Image>Adjustments menu.

Some of these, such as those concerned with converting colour images to black and white, we'll be visiting in detail in the relevant sections of the book, others we'll use as and when we need them in the step-by-step projects. But for now let's just go through them all in brief – some are so self-evident that they need little explanation. We'll work our way down the Adjustments menu, ignoring those we've covered already.

Color Balance...
Brightness/Contrast...
Two simple controls that have been around since the early days of Photoshop. The Color Balance sliders offer a simple way to change the overall red, green and blue mix in three broad tonal ranges (shadows, mid-tones and highlights), while the Brightness/Contrast control does just what its name suggests (the tool was revamped in CS3 and is now much less likely to produce awful results).

Black & White... (CS3+)
A new tool that offers a wide range of controls over the process of turning a colour image to black and white (see page 97). For the most part it supersedes the Channel Mixer (see page 95), which is also mainly used to fine-tune how the various colours in an image are mixed to create a grayscale output.

Desaturate
Exactly the same as reducing the Saturation to zero when using the Hue/Saturation adjustment. A quick way to remove colour.

Match Color (CS+)
A clever tool that allows you to match the colour balance across two images.

▼ CS4's new Vibrance adjustment, inherited from Lightroom, is a subtler way of increasing saturation (it doesn't affect colours that are already well-saturated).

▼ The Variations tool is the only purely visual adjustment in Photoshop; you simply keep clicking on the variation you prefer until you get the result you want.

The **Brightness/Contrast** adjustment may be a little crude but it's also very easy to use and does exactly what its name suggests.

The **Color Balance** controls are to colour what the Brightness/Contrast adjustments are to tone. Easy to use and relatively intuitive.

The only noteworthy thing about **Selective Color** is that you can adjust the colour balance of whites, neutrals and blacks, which is unusual.

The **Channel Mixer** is most commonly used to produce customized black and white conversions (see page 95).

Photoshop CS3's new **Black & White** tool offers a more sophisticated approach to Channel Mixing with a range of useful Presets.

The **Photo Filter** tool recreates conventional photographic filters and can be a quick way to remove mild colour casts.

Replace Color... (CS+)

Combines the Select>Color Range... and Hue/Saturation adjustment into a single step tool for, as the name suggests, replacing one colour with another.

Selective Color

A rather old and obscure tool that lets you change the colour balance of a particular band of colours.

Gradient Map

Maps the luminance of an image to a gradient going from the shadows (one end of the gradient) to the highlights (the other end of the gradient). One of the many ways to turn a colour image black and

white, or to add colourization to a mono image (see page 94).

Photo Filter (CS+)

A series of colour overlays that mimic and recreate the effect of conventional photographic colour-correction filters.

Exposure (CS2+)

A new way of brightening and darkening images that attempts to recreate the effect of changing the camera exposure.

Equalize

Evens out brightness across the frame; mainly used for correcting poor scans.

Invert

Makes a negative image.

Threshold

Creates a high-contrast two-tone image – the Threshold slider defines at what brightness the flip from black to white occurs (see page 122).

Posterize

Lets you reduce the number of tonal levels in an image for a 'pop art' effect (see page 118).

Variations

Makes tonal corrections visually by choosing from thumbnail variations (see opposite).

KEY PHOTO CORRECTIONS:
SHARPENING AND UNSHARP MASKING

Don't be fooled by the name; Unsharp Masking is a powerful and highly configurable tool for sharpening your digital images.

You may not need to sharpen every file you open in Photoshop but the chances are you will need to sharpen most of them. Many digital cameras produce slightly soft results 'out of camera', and common tasks such as resizing (for web use, for example) also reduce sharpness, requiring remedial action. Photoshop offers several sharpening tools, but they're all based on the same principle, and we're going to concentrate on the daddy of

them all, the Unsharp Mask (USM) filter (**Filter>Sharpen>Unsharp Mask**), which is a much more refined and controllable tool than the simple **Sharpen** and **Sharpen More** options. Newer versions of Photoshop also offer a refined Smart Sharpen filter (see page 66).

How It Works

Without going too deep, the USM filter increases the visual sharpness of an image by

Sharpening increases the contrast of edges to make them look sharper.

increasing the contrast of edges. It does this using a 'halo' (see above) that darkens the dark side of the edge, and brightens the light side.

UNSHARP MASKING BASICS

With a name as misleading as this, it's hardly surprising that Unsharp Masking (USM) is so widely misunderstood. But, USM is a very useful and easy-to-master tool.

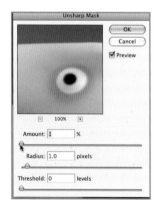

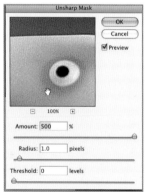

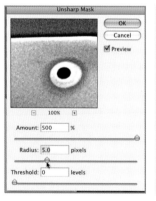

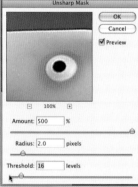

USM has three controls: **Amount** (the contrast of the edge), **Radius** (the size of the sharpening halo) and **Threshold** (protects areas of flat colour from sharpening).

As you increase the Amount the strength of the sharpening effect (the halo) increases. Generally we use low amounts with a high Radius setting and vice versa.

The Radius setting defines the size of the halo. Generally we're trying to match the Radius size to the smallest detail in the scene – too large and you'll lose fine detail.

The Threshold defines what is considered an edge for sharpening purposes and protects areas without detail. Usually left at zero unless the image is noisy.

WHAT SETTINGS TO USE?

The key to success with Unsharp Masking is to tailor the settings to the content of the picture you're working on. Here are some rough guidelines to get you started.

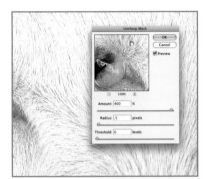

For very fine detail use a small Radius (0.3 to 0.6) and a high Amount (anything from 250% to 500%).

For low detail use a much lower Amount (in the 75 to 150% region) and a larger Radius (1.0 to 2.5 pixels).

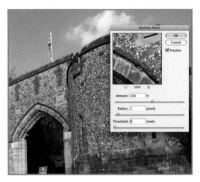

For images with a mixture of fine and low detail start with Photoshop's default settings (100%, 1.0 pixels).

THE VISUAL APPROACH

Start with the Amount set to 500% and a Radius setting in the rough area you think it should be. Now reduce the Radius setting until it matches the detail level in the image.

Once you're happy that the Radius is just below the point where it starts to obliterate fine detail, reduce the Amount slider until you have the amount of sharpening you want.

Flat areas of colour are left more or less untouched (which is where USM tends to be better than simple sharpening filters) It's important to remember that Unsharp Masking – like any sharpening filter – can't actually add detail to a shot, it simply enhances the appearance of sharpness, so it is of very limited value if the picture is out of focus.

USM Controls

There are three sliders in the USM dialog, and it's important to understand what each of them does if you're going to use this tool effectively.

Amount: the Amount slider defines how much the contrast around edges is increased.

Quick Tips

■ Never turn up the in-camera sharpening on your digital camera, as you can't Undo this kind of effect. It is, in fact, better to turn the in-camera sharpness down and do it yourself using Unsharp Masking.

■ Always work at 100% on-screen and remember that the effect of USM always looks stronger on-screen than it does in the printed image.

■ Always run sharpening filters after you've done any other image editing; it should be the last stage of the process. This is particularly important if you reduce or increase the size of the image for printing. If you reduce your images to a more manageable size for printing or emailing, a little Unsharp Masking will crisp up the softness you get after making such changes.

■ Sharpening of any kind will tend to exaggerate noise or other image artefacts. With poor-quality images use a lower amount of sharpening than you might normally.

Radius: this defines the size of the halo, in pixels. The bigger the Radius, the more pronounced the sharpening effect. Theoretically the Radius should be matched to the size of the smallest detail in the frame, but there's no magic formula for the right setting. Broadly speaking, finely detailed pictures (such as landscapes with foliage) use a small Radius (below 1.0), for images low in fine detail you can use a larger Radius.

Threshold: the last slider is different to the first two in that the higher the value you set it to, the less pronounced the sharpening effect is. The Threshold setting is designed to protect areas of flat colour from being sharpened, and it defines how different two tones have to be to be considered an

edge. For most images a Threshold of zero is fine, but if the image is noisy or the sharpening appears to be making the picture look grainy, you can increase it slightly (to 1 or 2). It's also useful for avoiding over-sharpening of skin texture in portraits.

What Settings?

The key to success with the Unsharp Mask lies in matching the Radius and Amount settings to the level of detail in the shot. For anything with fine detail a small Radius (below 1.0 pixels) and large Amount (over 200%) is usually the best approach – if the halo is too large it can actually reduce detail. For images without fine detail (those not featuring hair

or fur, for example) you may be better off using a larger Radius and a smaller Amount – especially if there is noise in the image (since the noise will be sharpened too).

You may find a setting that works for most of your shots (I nearly always start with an Amount of 200% and a Radius of 0.7, for example), but you should still experiment with the sliders (always viewing the preview image at 100% so you can really see what's happening). It is usually better to set the Radius first (based on the Amount of detail in the scene), then set the Amount to give the optimal sharpening, tweaking the Threshold if you get noisy speckles appearing in areas of flat colour (see The Visual Approach, page 65).

SMART SHARPEN (CS2+)

Introduced in Photoshop CS2, Smart Sharpen (Filter>Sharpen>Smart Sharpen) is a more sophisticated version of Unsharp Masking that often produces better results without the need for endless tweaking of parameters.

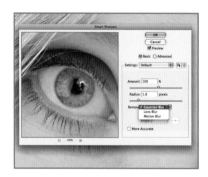

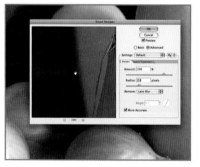

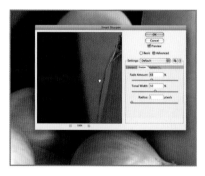

The Smart Sharpen tool has two modes; **Basic** and **Advanced**. In Basic mode you can choose from three different blur types. The **Gaussian Blur** option is very similar to using Unsharp Masking. The **Lens Blur** option is better for fine detail. **Motion Blur** tries (not terribly successfully) to remove blur caused by camera shake.

The main controls (**Amount** and **Radius**) are identical to those found in the Unsharp Mask tool (note there's no Threshold slider). Selecting the Advanced mode adds a couple of tabs (**Shadow** and **Highlight**). These allow you to **Fade** (reduce) the sharpening effect in the shadow or highlight portions of your image.

The **Shadow** option is the most useful; strong sharpening increases the visibility of noise in shadows. By reducing the sharpening in the shadow areas (where noise is worst) you can sharpen the image without making the noise situation any worse.

Sharpening With Layers

Inevitably, there will be times when you'll want to apply sharpening selectively (to the eyes but not the skin of a portrait, for example) or to be able to use sharpening in a non-destructive (reversible) way. Photoshop's new Smart Filters (see below), introduced in CS3, are ideal, but they're by no means the only option, and there are plenty of alternative techniques that can be used with older versions too.

Perhaps the most obvious approach is to simply create a duplicate layer and sharpen that; you can then add a Layer Mask (masking the areas of the frame you don't want sharpening) as well as alter the Opacity of the sharpened layer to reduce the effect overall. A more sophisticated approach is High Pass sharpening (see page 68).

The simplest way to apply sharpening in a non-destructive and selective manner is to sharpen a duplicate layer and use a Layer Mask.

SMART FILTERS (CS3+)

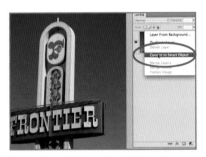

Photoshop CS3 saw the debut of **Smart Filters** (filters that can be edited after they've been applied). Start by right-clicking on a layer and choosing **Convert to Smart Object**.

Now run the **Unsharp Mask** filter (or any other filter for that matter). Use whatever settings you wish but don't worry too much – you're filtering in a non-destructive manner now!

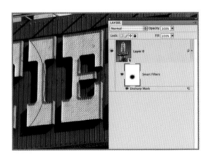

Now look at the **Layers** palette; the Smart Filter is attached to the layer and has a Layer Mask so you can paint out the sharpening effect. You can delete the mask – or the filter itself – at any time.

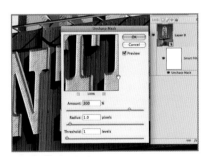

Double-click on the filter name to change the settings. You can also adjust the Opacity and Blending Mode of the filter by double-clicking on the little sliders icon to the right of the filter name.

HIGH PASS SHARPENING

An alternative non-destructive way of sharpening using layers – and one many professional photographers swear by – is High Pass Sharpening. Here's how you do it.

Start by creating a duplicate of your image in a new layer (Ctrl-J / ⌘-J is the easiest way).

Change the Blending Mode of the upper layer to **Overlay**.

Choose the **High Pass** filter (**Filter>Other>High Pass**).

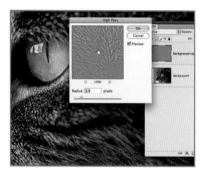

When the High Pass dialog appears select a **Radius** that matches the level of detail in your image. A smallish Radius is perfect for the fine detail in the fur in this shot.

Click OK to apply the High Pass filter. You can fine-tune the strength of the sharpening effect by reducing the Opacity of the upper layer.

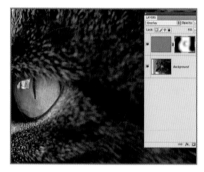

And because it's a separate layer you can also add a **Layer Mask** (see pages 38-43). This allows you to reduce or remove the sharpening effect from selected areas of the frame.

By now I hope you've come to appreciate that there's a lot more to sharpening than simply selecting the **Sharpen** or **Sharpen More** option from the **Filter>Sharpen** menu. If there's one thing you should take away from this section it's that there are no blanket settings that produce the best results from every image; whichever sharpening tool you use – you need to tailor the settings to the image itself.

Aside from this basic fact – that sharpening settings need to be matched to the individual image being worked on at the time – the important things to remember can be summed up in a few simple principles.

First is that the Radius setting needs to be matched to the level of detail in your image: if it's too high you can start to reduce detail. Second is that you should, as a rule, make sharpening the last step in any image-editing process. This is particularly true if you are resizing images or printing (if you are producing small prints you should ideally reduce the image size then sharpen).

Thirdly, and finally, remember that there are plenty of techniques and tools that allow you to sharpen an image selectively, whether to avoid exaggerating noise in shadows or to protect skin texture from sharpening.

KEY PHOTO CORRECTIONS:
CROPPING AND STRAIGHTENING

Whether you're trying to improve composition, remove unwanted elements or correct a wonky horizon, the Crop tool offers a fast and easy fix.

It is, perhaps, the single most basic image edit available to the digital photographer, yet cropping is also one of the most powerful – capable of transforming a mediocre photo into a masterpiece, and of rescuing the most unpromising shot from the Recycle Bin. There are times when trimming away the edges of a photo can really make or break it. Photoshop's Crop tool (keyboard shortcut: C) is actually a surprisingly powerful one, capable of rotating, resizing, trimming and even distorting an image in a single click. You'll be using it a lot, so now is as good a time as any to get to know it.

USING THE CROP TOOL

Select the **Crop** tool (or press C) and click and drag to define the area you want to trim. An overlay shows the areas to be trimmed. The cropped area can be resized by clicking on and pulling any of the handles (corners and mid-points of each side).

You can also rotate the crop. Position the cursor just outside the crop area, near a handle, and you'll see the cursor icon change as shown here. You can always move the cropped area around the frame by clicking inside it and dragging.

Now when you click and drag the cropped area will rotate, allowing you to correct the rather skewed horizon in this shot quickly.

To accept the crop simply press the **Enter** key or double-click inside the cropped area.

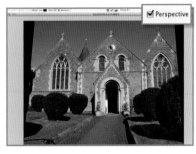

Click on the **Perspective** option and you can pull the corners in to create a non-rectangular crop area.

This allows you to correct perspective distortion in a single click – perfect for those 'falling over' building shots.

CROP TOOL OPTIONS

With an active crop, the overlay (which shows the areas to be trimmed away) can be changed in both **Color** and **Opacity**.

You can set a crop size (**Width** and **Height**) and **Resolution** before you use the Crop tool - useful for quickly resizing an image prior to printing.

With an active crop you can choose to **Hide** rather than **Delete** areas outside the crop. The latter is the same as reducing the Canvas Size, and means areas outside the crop are not lost.

STRAIGHTENING BEFORE CROPPING

Like most things in Photoshop there are several ways to straighten an image - some of which allow more accuracy than using the Crop tool in a purely visual manner.

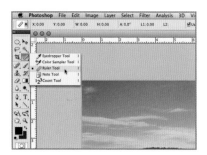

To get perfectly straight horizons you need to measure the angles, for which you need the **Ruler** tool (it's hidden under the Eyedropper in the tool palette). You'll also need the **Info** palette, so press F8 to bring it up.

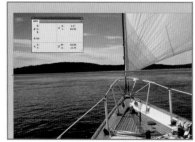

Use the Ruler tool to draw a line across the horizon of your wonky image (highlighted here in red). You'll see the angle of the line appearing on the Info palette.

Now choose Image>Rotate Canvas> Arbitrary.... If you've done nothing since the last step the angle will already have been filled in for you, otherwise use the value from the Info palette. Click OK.

The horizon is now, as it should be, perfectly horizontal. Now you'll need to use the Crop tool to trim away the white edges.

Unlocked Layers can also be rotated using the **Transform** tool (Edit> Transform>Rotate or Edit>Free Transform).

If you are rotating an image in this way, you may want to temporarily turn on the **Grid** (View>Show>Grid). Note that you can use the Grid with the Crop tool too.

CHAPTER FIVE

COMMON PHOTO TASKS

Now we've covered the basics of Photoshop's most useful tools and techniques, it's time to start putting all that theory into practice with some real-world projects. This chapter looks at some of the edits and corrections commonly applied to digital photographs, and you will pick up some tips on Photoshop's more advanced tools along the way.

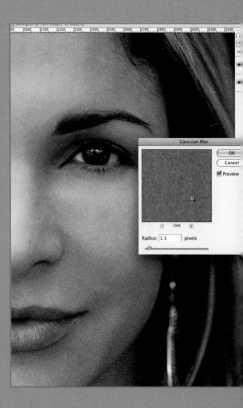

Although Photoshop is used for everything from computer games graphics and movie special effects to forensic image analysis - and a great deal in between - it would be fair to guess that the most common application is for that with which its name has become synonymous; the editing and correction of photographs.

We've already looked at brightness, contrast, colour, sharpness and cropping corrections - the everyday essentials of the digital darkroom - but even in the hands of a beginner Photoshop is capable of much, much more. And while there's

no substitute for getting everything perfect when you press the shutter, in reality this isn't always the case, and in fact is rarely possible. This is where a little helping hand from Photoshop can transform a mediocre snapshot into something really special.

Given the sheer size of Photoshop's feature set and the almost limitless possibilities it offers, we can only really scratch the surface here. But, I hope these projects and guides will at least provide a starting point for editing your own photographs and for sorting out some of the most common problems you will face.

STEP-BY-STEP: QUICK FIX FOR A DULL DAY
🕐 10 MINUTES
▦ EASY

START HERE

⚙ You'll need a basic grasp of Layers, Masks and tonal controls for this simple project. It will work in any version of Photoshop.

🔍 **Also See:**
Adjustment Layers: page 44
Levels and Histograms: page 48
Hue/Saturation: page 60
Layers and Masks: pages 29-46

A miserable day usually spells disaster for photographs; here's how to pull something out of the dullest shot.

We've all done it; taken a day trip somewhere new to shoot pictures, only to have our plans scuppered by the weather. If you're stuck with a load of shots that are dull as dishwater, worry not; here's a quick fix in a few steps – including the digital version of the old faithful graduated tint filter.

Start Image

End Result

STEP 01

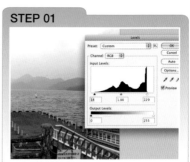

Let's start by fixing the lack of contrast. Obviously every shot will need a slightly different treatment; here I'm using **Levels** (Crtl-L / ⌘-L) to set the white and black points (see page 49).

STEP 02

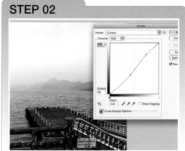

Here, I'm using **Curves** (Crtl-M / ⌘-M) to increase the contrast of the shadows and mid-tones just a little more, while protecting the highlights in the sky area (see page 58).

STEP 03

To darken the sky we're going to use an Adjustment Layer (page 44). Choose **Layer>New Adjustment Layer>Levels** (or pick Levels from the pop-out menu at the bottom of the Layers palette, as shown here).

STEP 04

When the **Levels** dialog appears move the grey (Gamma) slider to the right until the clouds look nice and distinct. Here, I've also moved the black point slider a little to the right. At this point the whole image looks too dark.

STEP 05

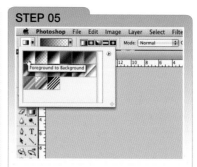

Press D to restore the default Foreground and Background Colors. Now select the **Gradient** tool (G) and select a **Foreground to Background** gradient (click on the arrow next to the gradient in the Options bar).

STEP 06

Select the Adjustment Layer's mask (circled above). Click just below the horizon and release the mouse button just above the horizon (see arrow above). You should see the lower half of the image lighten up again.

STEP 07

Most overcast shots are lacking colour, so it's worth trying a Saturation boost. Choose **Image> Adjustments>Hue/ Saturation** and increase the Saturation to around +30.

STEP 08

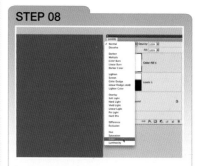

To add a graduated tint, first add a Color Fill Layer (**Layer>New Fill Layer >Color Fill...**) and choose a colour when the dialog appears (I've gone for a blue tone). Change the Blending Mode of the new layer to **Color**.

STEP 09

To restrict the colour effect to the upper half of the frame you'll need once again to add a gradient to the Fill Layer's mask (as per step 06). You'll also want to reduce the Opacity of the Color Fill Layer.

STEP 10

The last step in this particular project is to fine-tune the tone (here lightening the mid-tones slightly using **Levels**) and to sharpen using the **Unsharp Mask** filter (see page 64), and we're done.

Version Differences

Adjustment Layers
Photoshop CS4 introduces a new non-modal way of controlling Adjustment Layer settings. Although the

Adjustment Layers themselves work in exactly the same way, the actual adjustments are now done using the new Adjustments palette, which appears as soon as you add an Adjustment Layer.

COMMON PHOTO TASKS:
REMOVING BLEMISHES

From dust spots to birthmarks, tourists to telegraph poles, there are countless things we'd like to airbrush out of our pictures. Fortunately Photoshop makes it easy.

Back in early 1992, when I first started using Photoshop, my first big 'wow' moment came when I saw the Rubber Stamp tool in action. For although skilled artists have been airbrushing photographs ever since Victorian sitters first complained about unflattering Daguerreotypes, there really is no real-world darkroom equivalent for the Rubber Stamp and its related tools.

Yet what it does is actually very simple; the Rubber Stamp tool (often referred to as the Clone tool because that's what

it does) lets you to paint over one area of an image with pixels from a different area of the same image (or a different image if you desire). It acts in the same way as the Paint Brush. You can change the shape and size of the brush itself by selecting any one of the Presets in the Brushes palette.

The most common use for the Rubber Stamp tool is to remove blemishes or other unwanted elements from photographs. From spots and wrinkles on portraits, to dust and scratches on scanned images, to telephone wires,

tourists or parked cars in scenery shots, Photoshop's amazing cloning abilities allow you to paint away blemishes seamlessly with a few brush strokes. The newer tools – Patch, Healing and Spot Healing – are specifically designed to make the process of removing blemishes such as spots and dust even easier by matching the cloned pixels to the target area automatically. We'll be looking at all Photoshop's cloning and healing tools over the next couple of pages, then putting them to use in a couple of sample projects.

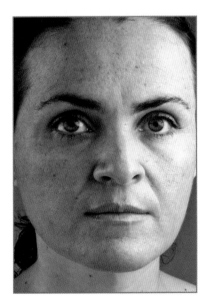

We're not all blessed with supermodel skin - not even supermodels. Few sitters want a portrait that shows too many blemishes, wrinkles or dark rings under the eyes.

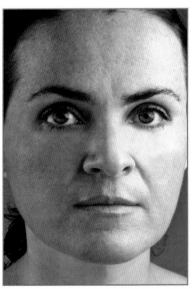

The Rubber Stamp tool allows you to clone pixels from one area of the frame over another area, thereby removing the blemishes in a totally seamless manner.

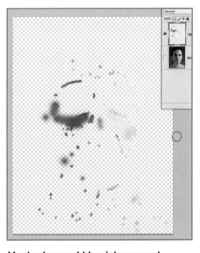

Most advanced blemish removal projects such as this one take advantage of Photoshop's ability to clone from one layer on to another. The screenshot above shows the layer I created during the process of removing the blemishes from the image on the left.

RUBBER STAMP TOOL BASICS

The idea behind the Rubber Stamp tool is simple; it paints over one area of an image (the 'target') with pixels from another area (the 'source').

The starting point of any cloning process is to define the source pixels (those you're going to paint with). In Photoshop you do this by selecting the **Rubber Stamp** tool (keyboard shortcut: S) and holding down the Alt (⌥) key as you click the mouse.

Once you've Alt/⌥-clicked to set the source pixels simply click and move the mouse like any other Paint tool to paint with them. In this, and all the examples to follow, I'm using a red circle to indicate source pixels, a yellow circle to indicate the target area.

As you paint with the Rubber Stamp the source point is indicated with a small cross hair. Here I'm using a bit of clean sky to paint away a dust spot from a digital SLR shot.

As you master the Rubber Stamp tool you'll be able to try more and more ambitious airbrush jobs. Here I'm going to attempt to remove a person from a scene without leaving a trace.

With careful alignment of the source point (particularly when cloning edges) it is possible to convincingly paint over any areas you want to remove in almost any scene.

By working slowly and carefully even a complex background such as this can be cloned to cover any unwanted elements in the scene.

Rubber Stamp Options

Like all Photoshop's tools the Rubber Stamp has several options – shown in the Options bar just below the main menu bar (if you can't see it choose Window>Options). Those specific to the Rubber Stamp are the Aligned and Sample options. Older versions of Photoshop simply have a Use All Layers tick box, later versions give you the Current Layer, Current & Below and All Layers options. In multi-layered documents these define whether the Rubber Stamp only clones pixels from the current layer. Use the All Layers option for non-destructive cloning on to a transparent 'clone layer' (see page 78 for a step-by-step guide). If the Aligned option is off the clone source remains the same until

you re-sample (Alt/⌥-click again). If you turn the Aligned option on, the clone source stays a constant distance from wherever you paint. Which mode you use depends on the circumstances; non-aligned is particularly useful for covering large areas with a small sample of original texture, but can lead to noticeable repetitive patterns.

HEALING TOOLS

Designed to take the strain out of blemish removal, Photoshop's healing tools are powerful, fast and easy to use.

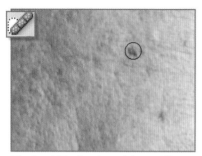

The **Spot Healing Brush** is used like any other brush tool – you can set the size and hardness using the Brushes palette. Leave the Source option set to **Sampled** and the mode **Normal**.

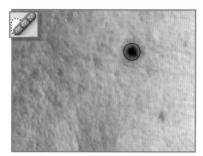

The pixels that will be healed turn black as you paint – here I'm simply clicking once on the blemish with a soft-edged brush sized just large enough to cover it.

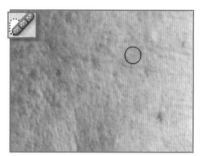

Photoshop automatically picks source pixels from nearby and – with simple textures such as skin – almost always produces perfect results.

You can also paint with the Spot Healing Brush – great for removing anything from wrinkles to telephone wires. Here, I'm using a smaller brush so I just cover the line I'm removing.

The Spot Healing Brush can get things wrong if there's not enough flat texture nearby to sample, but if you use as small a brush as possible, and follow the blemish as closely as you can it usually works.

After a couple of moments the Spot Healing Brush has done its magic and the wrinkle has gone. If the Spot Healing Brush gets confused and uses the wrong source pixels, you'll need the **Healing Brush**.

Healing Tools

Photoshop 7.0 saw the introduction of the Healing and Patch tools (later joined by the Spot Healing tool in CS2). These supercharged versions of the Rubber Stamp tool offer an easier, faster and more intelligent way to remove minor blemishes in what can literally be a single click.

Although they work in a similar way to the Rubber Stamp tool, the

Healing tools don't just replace the pixels in the areas you paint with the source (sampled) pixels. Instead they attempt to match the texture, lighting and shading of the target pixels to the source pixels for a seamless blend. And a fairly good job they make of it too. See the top of the page for a quick rundown of what each tool does.

The Spot Healing Brush is the simplest way to remove small blemishes – such as dust spots

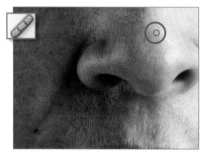

Like the Rubber Stamp, the **Healing Brush Tool** lets you choose your own source pixels to sample. Again Alt/⌥-click to set the source point.

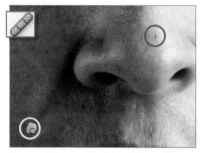

Now paint over the blemish; you'll see the source pixels appear as you paint.

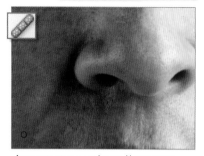

As soon as you release the mouse button Photoshop automatically blends the detail of the source pixels with the tone and colour of the target area. The result is seamless.

To use the **Patch Tool** first draw a selection around the blemish you wish you remove (I'm using this eyebrow as a rather dramatic example).

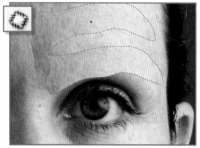

Drag the selection to an area of texture you wish to use as the source for the patching. As shown above you'll see the source pixels appear inside your original selection as you move. Let go of the mouse button.

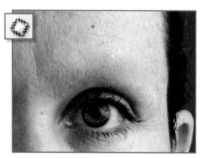

The selected area will be filled and tonally matched for a perfect blend. The **Patch Destination** option allows you to flip the way the tool works (so that you drag the source pixels on to the blemish).

- from areas of relatively even texture (such as skin or skies), and as it doesn't require you to Alt/⌥-click first (the tool picks its own source pixels to sample), it really does offer one-click healing. The Healing Brush is used in exactly the same way as the Rubber Stamp tool (Alt/⌥-clicking to define source pixels). The Patch tool works as a combination of the Healing Brush and the Lasso Selection tool and is ideal for

removing larger blemishes. The Healing tools work well enough to be considered your first port of call when removing blemishes, but like all automatic tools there are going to be times when they get things wrong, at which point you'll need to go back to the Rubber Stamp. It's also worth getting to know the various options available for each of the tools; the default settings often work well but they aren't foolproof.

Rubber Stamp Tip

As the Rubber Stamp tool works like the Paint Brush, you can alter the shape, size and softness using the Brushes palette. Use smaller, harder brushes to clone over more detailed areas, and a larger, softer brush for more expansive areas.

You can use the square bracket keys [and] to quickly change brush size, while Shift-[/ Shift-] will change the hardness of the brush.

REMOVING UNWANTED ELEMENTS
 40 MINUTES
INTERMEDIATE

After our quick tour of Photoshop's Cloning and Healing tools let's try a simple Rubber Stamping exercise.

 START HERE

Only two tools are used in this project; the Rubber Stamp (keyboard shortcut: S) and, if you make a mistake, the Eraser (keyboard shortcut: E). You'll need a basic grasp of Layers and Brushes too.

 Also See:
Removing Blemishes: page 74
Layers: page 30

I say simple, but the removal of the ugly barbed-wire fence from this shot is actually rather involved; there's lots of detail and plenty of edges behind it, so we're going to be putting our cloning skills to the test. The great thing is we can do the whole thing with a single tool: the Rubber Stamp.

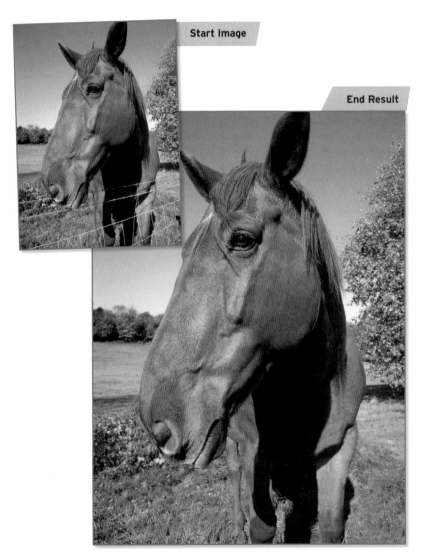

Start Image

End Result

STEP 01

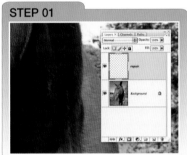

For a job this fiddly we really need to use a clone layer, so start by creating a new transparent layer (**Layer>New>Layer**). Make sure this layer is active by clicking on it in the Layers palette.

STEP 02

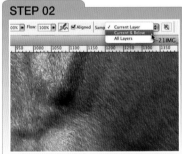

Select the Rubber Stamp tool (or press S). Then go to the Options bar at the top of the screen and choose **Current & Below** from the Sample menu (*pre-CS3:* tick the **Sample All Layers** option).

STEP 03

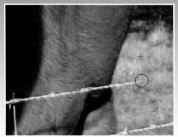

We'll start with the easy areas, where there's only grass behind the wire. Pick a small, soft brush from the Brushes palette and Alt/⌥-click to set the source point. Now start to paint over the wire.

STEP 04

It's easy to accidentally create repeating patterns (by repeatedly cloning from the same small area). Go back and paint over any such areas a second time.

STEP 05

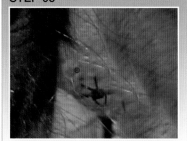

You'll need to zoom in to 100% view and use a very small brush size for really fiddly areas. If you go wrong simply switch to the **Eraser** tool (press E) and delete the offending pixels.

STEP 06

Remember that we're cloning on to a separate layer, so you can always hide the upper layer to see the original image.

STEP 07

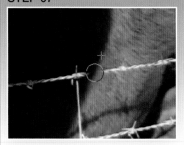

Take special care when cloning edges to ensure they line up. You need to Alt/⌥-click in the right place (right on the edge) and you may need to try a few times before you get it right.

STEP 08

Once you're happy with the result flatten the image (**Layer>Flatten Image**) and save it as a new file.

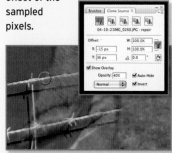

QUICK 'PERFECT SKIN' MAKEOVER

 40 MINUTES
ADVANCED

Anyone can have 'cover girl' perfect skin courtesy of this relatively simple Photoshop makeover.

START HERE

 This project is more about your mouse skill than the use of particularly advance Photoshop tools or techniques. You'll need a basic grasp of Layers, Masks and Brush tools.

 Also See:
Removing Blemishes: page 74
Layers and Masks: pages 29-46

Have you ever wondered why every celebrity and model appearing on magazine covers and in adverts looks like they have the perfect skin of a newborn baby? The answer is, of course, they've had a complete makeover thanks to Photoshop. Here's a quick step-by-step guide to getting the same results with your own portraits. It's not a complicated technique and shouldn't take too long.

Start Image

End Result

STEP 01

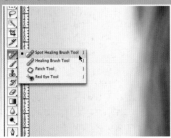

Start by removing the most obvious blemishes (pimples, spots, heavy wrinkles, facial hair and so on). I'm starting with the **Spot Healing Brush** as this allows one-click fixes for smaller blemishes.

STEP 02

Work your way around the image (zoomed in) and remove the most obvious blemishes. Here, I'm using the **Healing Brush** to remove plucked eyebrow stubble.

STEP 03

Use the Healing Brush to remove any particularly deep wrinkles. Don't worry too much about getting it perfect; you just want to get rid of the most prominent blemishes.

STEP 04

Here's my example when I've finished the initial clean-up process. Note that I've used the **Patch** tool to cover the dark areas under the eyes. Now duplicate the Background Layer (press Ctrl-J / ⌘-J)

STEP 05

With the upper (duplicate) layer active choose Filter>Blur>Gaussian Blur. If you're using version CS2 or higher you could also use a **Smart Layer** rather than a duplicate layer (see panel, right).

STEP 06

Choose a blur **Radius** large enough to completely remove all texture from the skin – this will depend on the size of the image, but expect it to be in the 30-70 pixel range.

STEP 07

Add a **Layer Mask** to the upper (blurred) layer by clicking on the icon at the bottom of the Layers palette.

STEP 08

Click on the Layer Mask thumbnail and make sure the **Foreground Color** is set to black (press D to reset if it isn't). Now start to paint on to the mask all the areas you want to remain sharp. You can do this pretty roughly at first – we'll fine-tune later.

Smart Layers

CS2 **CS3** **CS4**

Smart Filter Technique
With Photoshop CS2 and later this project can be done non-destructively using a single layer.

Start by right-clicking on the Background Layer and choosing **Convert to Smart Object**.

Now run the **Gaussian Blur** filter as outlined in steps 05-06. You'll see a Smart Filter with a Layer Mask appear in the Layers palette.

Edit this mask using the **Brush** tool as described in steps 08-11.

The advantage of using a Smart Filter is that you can, if you wish, go back and change the Gaussian Blur settings at any time – and reduce its Opacity. Double-clicking on the right-hand icon below the mask opens the Blending and Opacity options for the filter. Double-clicking on the filter name opens the filter dialog and lets you change its settings.

STEP 09

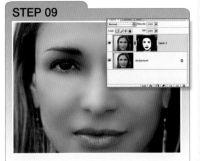

After you've painted on to the mask you should see something like this; the skin area is totally smooth. You'll probably notice that the edges look too soft, so we need to fine-tune the mask on the upper layer.

STEP 10

Zoom in and use a smaller brush to make sure all the edges are sharp. Use black paint to reveal more of the underlying layer (the original) and white paint to reveal more of the blurred skin layer.

STEP 11

Work around the image and get it as clean as you can. You need to take care – and use a smaller brush – around the eyebrows and eyelashes.

STEP 12

Unless you want a totally plastic skin tone (which is, of course, how some magazines treat their models) this is about as far as you need to go – the problem areas (around the eyebrows and eyelashes) will soon disappear.

STEP 13

To get a more realistic skin texture reduce the Opacity of the top layer to somewhere between 40 and 65%. I've chosen 55%, which allows some of the skin pores to show through without losing the nice smooth look.

STEP 14

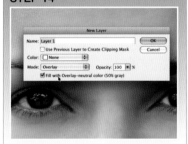

Now to even out the texture across the frame. Start by choosing **Layer> New>Layer**. When the New Layer dialog appears choose **Overlay** mode and tick the **Fill with Overlay-neutral color** option. Click OK.

Technique Tip: Whitening Teeth

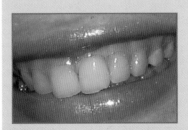

Nobody likes to see their teeth looking anything less than pearly white in a photo. Fortunately it's easy to fix in Photoshop. Start by drawing a rough selection.

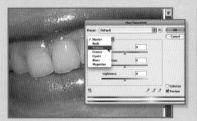

Next choose **Image>Adjustments> Hue/Saturation** and select **Yellows** from the **Edit** drop-down menu.

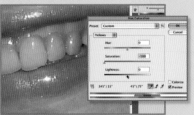

Reduce the **Saturation** to -100 (don't worry that it looks black and white – it won't stay that way).

STEP 15

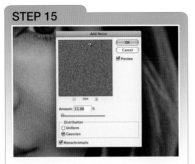

With the new layer active choose **Filter>Noise>Add Noise**. Set the Amount to around 10–15% and select the **Gaussian** and **Monochromatic** options. You should see the noise appear as an overlay on your image.

STEP 16

For a slightly softer, less grainy effect run a gentle Gaussian Blur filter (**Filter>Blur >Gaussian Blur**) of just 1 or 2 pixels on the noise layer you just created.

STEP 17

Finally, reduce the Opacity of the noise layer until you're happy with the effect (the amount needed will depend totally on how smooth you left the skin in step 13).

STEP 18

You can easily add digital makeup by creating a new empty layer, changing its Blending Mode to **Color** and its Opacity to around 50%, then painting using a soft brush with the colour you want to use.

Quick Tips

Even Out Skin Tone

The method mentioned in step 18 for adding digital makeup can also be used to sort out uneven skin tone. Simply create a transparent layer, set it to Color mode at 50% Opacity and paint using your chosen skin tone over the offending areas.

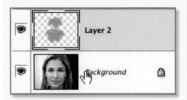

Reduce Skin Redness

Whether it's due to dryness, sunburn or lighting conditions, red skin is rarely flattering in a photograph.

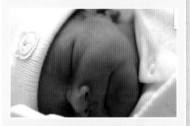

To remove it quickly first choose **Image>Adjustments>Hue/ Saturation** and choose **Reds** from the edit menu at the top of the dialog. Move the Hue slider very slightly to the right (which makes tones a little more yellow) and reduce the Saturation until the skin tone looks more natural.

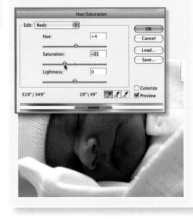

To narrow the band of colour you're desaturating (so it only affects the teeth) use the sliders at the bottom of the dialog box. Experiment until the gums are no longer affected.

Finally, reduce the **Lightness** setting slightly and turn the Saturation back up until the tooth tone looks natural again.

PORTRAIT FIX: REMOVING RED-EYE
⏱ 5 MINUTES
📊 EASY

START HERE

⚙ If you're using Photoshop CS2 or later removing red-eye is usually a matter of one or two clicks. The technique described in steps 03-06 is for earlier versions or for when the automatic tool doesn't work.

🔍 **Also See:**
Hue/Saturation: page 60
Levels and Histograms: page 48

Here's how to fix one of the most common portrait problems; red-eye caused by on-camera flash.

Red-eye is the curse of compact cameras, turning even the most angelic subjects into demons. Recent versions of Photoshop offer one-click removal, but if you're using an older version fear not, there is an easy alternative technique that takes a few more clicks but works a treat.

STEP 01

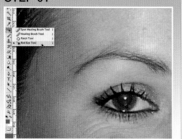

If you're using Photoshop CS2 or later you'll find a dedicated **Red-Eye** tool in with the Healing tools (click on the **Healing Brush** tool and hold down the mouse button until the flyout menu appears).

STEP 02

Using the tool couldn't be easier - just click on each of the eyes in turn; the rest is fully automatic. If you don't get the results you expect, Undo and try a different **Pupil Size** setting (on the Options bar).

STEP 03

There are lots of ways to remove red-eye in earlier versions; here's my favourite. Use the **Elliptical Marquee** to draw a circle round the pupil of the eye and **Feather** the selection by a few pixels (**Select>Modify>Feather**).

STEP 04

Choose **Image>Adjustment>Hue/ Saturation** and pick **Reds** from the drop-down menu. You can fine-tune the colour range by clicking on the image inside the red-eye.

STEP 05

Reduce the Saturation slider all the way to -100. This should remove every trace of red from the pupil.

STEP 06

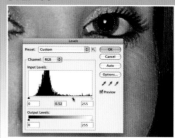

Finally to darken the pupil choose **Image>Adjustments>Levels** and move the middle (grey) slider over to the right until you're happy with the result.

DIGITAL CAMERA FIX: COLOUR FRINGES

 5 MINUTES
EASY

START HERE

 This technique uses Adjustment Layers and Masks and you'll need a basic understanding of how the Hue/Saturation adjustments work.

 Also See:
Hue/Saturation: page 60
Layers and Masks: pages 29-46
Camera Raw Basics: page 154

If you've got a fringe around your foliage fear not; getting rid of it is a simple job for Photoshop.

Many digital cameras suffer from an optical effect which produces (usually purple) fringes around high-contrast edges (back-lit foliage being the most common culprit). You can't get rid of it completely but minimizing the visibility of the colour fringes only takes a couple of minutes.

STEP 01

Start by creating a new Hue/Saturation Adjustment Layer (use the icon at the bottom of the Layers palette or choose **Layer>New Adjustment Layer>Hue/Saturation**).

STEP 02

You're trying to get rid of purple fringes so choose **Magentas** from the drop-down menu. This means any changes you make will only affect a narrow band of colours.

STEP 03

To perfectly match the colour range to the purple fringing, click on one of the fringe areas on the image itself.

STEP 04

Now reduce the Saturation until the fringes disappear (well, strictly speaking, until the colour is removed from them).

STEP 05

If there are other purple areas in the frame that you don't want removing, you'll need to paint on the Adjustment Layer's mask (with black paint) to bring them back.

Quick Tip

To remove chromatic aberrations right-click on your image in Bridge and choose **Open in Camera Raw....** Click on the **Lens Corrections** tab and use the **Chromatic Aberration** sliders (see page 156 for more on Adobe Camera Raw).

DIGITAL CAMERA FIX: NOISE REDUCTION

 5-10 MINUTES
 INTERMEDIATE

Image noise - digital grain - is a problem faced by all digital camera users at one point or another.

Digital camera noise comes in two forms; luminance noise (which makes the detail in the image look grainy) and chroma noise (which produces random dots or patches of colour across the frame. Of the two it is the latter that tends to be the bigger problem - we can live with a little granular texture (as we did in the days of film), but colour noise looks unnatural and can be seen even in relatively small prints. Any attempt to reduce luminance noise also reduces real image detail, something that's rarely

desirable. For these reasons we tend to want to concentrate on removing colour noise.

Photoshop CS2 introduced a dedicated noise reduction filter (**Filter>Noise>Reduce Noise**) that does a pretty good job and can - if you click on the Advanced option - be applied to the colour channels. It also allows you to treat luminance and chroma noise separately. If you're using an older version of Photoshop - or want more control over colour noise reduction, try the technique below.

CS2 & LATER

To restrict the **Reduce Noise** filter to colour noise only, set the **Strength** to maximum, **Preserve Details** to 80-100% and **Reduce Color Noise** to 100%. There is still some loss of detail, but it's minimal.

REDUCING COLOUR NOISE USING LAB MODE

STEP 01

One way to reduce colour noise without losing too much detail is to work in LAB mode (**Image>Mode Lab Color**). This technique is also useful for older versions of Photoshop. If it's not already on-screen, open the Channels palette (**Window>Channels**).

STEP 02

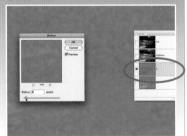

Click on the **a** channel in the Channels palette and choose **Filter>Noise> Median**. Use a Radius of between 4 and 10 pixels (depending on how strong the colour noise in the image is). Do the same thing for the **b** channel and sharpen the **Lightness** channel.

TIP

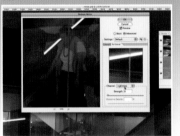

You can also use the **Reduce Noise** filter in LAB mode. The **Advanced** option now allows you to apply noise reduction at different levels to the colour channels (**a** and **b**) while leaving the Lightness channel untouched.

USING CURVES TO FIX WHITE BALANCE
 5 MINUTES
ADVANCED

Get rid of unwanted colour casts the intelligent way.

START HERE

 This is a useful technique to learn if none of the automatic tools produce the result you want. Note that if you shoot Raw it's better to fix white balance at the point you develop the Raw file.

Also See:
Curves: page 54
Using Camera Raw: page 153

Photoshop's automatic colour correction tools work well, but they're far from foolproof. When all else fails, using Curves you can remove colour casts and white balance problems numerically – without having to rely on the accuracy of your computer screen or your own eyesight.

STEP 01

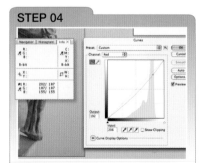

Start by opening the **Info** window (press F8). This will allow you to make changes to the colours in the image numerically, rather than by eye. Now select the **Color Sampler** tool.

STEP 02

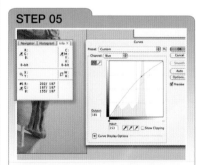

Click with the Color Sampler on the image in an area you want to be neutral grey. You'll see the RGB values for the sampler point appear on the Info palette. The values here are far from neutral (R202, G187, B155).

STEP 03

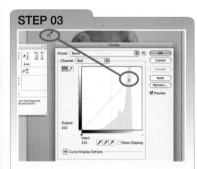

Now Choose Image>Adjustments> Curves. Pick **Red** from the **Channel** menu and click in the image near the sample point. A dot will appear on the graph to show you where on the curve this colour lies.

STEP 04

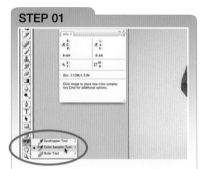

Click on the curve at this point and drag down until the R value on the Info palette matches the G value (187). The Info palette usefully shows both before and after values for the changes you make.

STEP 05

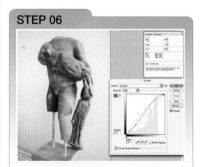

Now to do the same with the **Blue** channel – in this case the blue curve needs to be lifted to meet the green value of 187. All three channels now read the same value so the back wall is now neutral grey.

STEP 06

Finally, increase the overall contrast of the image using the RGB curve. You can also correct colour separately for the highlights and shadows by placing more than one Color Sampler on the image in question.

COMMON PHOTO TASKS:
LOCALIZED EXPOSURE AND CONTRAST

We've already covered many of Photoshop's brightness and contrast adjustment techniques. But what if you need to restrict the effect to only part of the image?

Just as photographers would vary the exposure given to different areas of a print using dodging and burning, Photoshop allows you – in many varied ways – to apply tonal changes at different levels to different parts of an image.

There are several reasons you might want to do this. The limited dynamic range in a typical RGB JPEG means there are always going to be some images that simply can't be corrected satisfactorily using a single overall adjustment. A typical example is a landscape with large amounts of sky, where correcting the foreground causes the sky to be over-brightened (losing all detail) and vice versa – correcting the sky leaves the foreground too dark.

There are also plenty of purely aesthetic reasons for selectively lightening or darkening areas of an image, particularly those taken in less than perfect lighting conditions.

The simplest way to apply a localized adjustment is via an Adjustment Layer (see page 44), using the layer's mask to restrict the changes to the areas you choose. We've already seen this in action in the quick-fix project on page 72. For small jobs – simple portrait fixes such as brightening the whites of eyes or lightening teeth, for example – the Dodge and Burn tools are quick and relatively easy to use, but once you get into more involved localized corrections the advantage of

Photoshop's Dodge and Burn tools allow you to respectively lighten or darken selected areas of an image using brush strokes.

working with Layers and Masks becomes obvious.

For scenes with a very wide range of brightness levels that cannot be captured in a single exposure, the only solution is to shoot more than one photograph, each at a different exposure level. These can then be combined back into a single image using a variety of techniques (see opposite). This is the basis of High Dynamic Range (HDR) photography.

USING AN ADJUSTMENT LAYER

By far the most flexible way to apply localized adjustments is with an Adjustment Layer and its mask. In this case Levels is being used to darken the water without darkening the statue. As always, painting with black on the mask protects those areas from the effect of the adjustment.

A variation on the Adjustment Layers technique is to create a duplicate layer and brighten (or darken) that. You can then use a Layer Mask to hide the areas you want to 'show through' from the original image.

As covered on page 53, more recent versions of Photoshop offer a useful **Shadow/Highlight** adjustment, which can be very useful for quickly lifting excessively dark shadow areas without blowing out the highlights.

Photoshop CS2 introduced a new **Merge to HDR** tool. This blends images taken at different exposures into a single high dynamic range (HDR) image.

COMBINING TWO EXPOSURES

One of the easiest ways of overcoming the limited dynamic range of most digital cameras blowing out sky detail is to take two shots and combine them using Photoshop when you get back to the computer.

Here are two shots of the same scene; one metered for the sky, the other for the foreground. No single shot could get all the tonal detail I wanted across the frame.

Drag one image on to the other using the Move tool to create a new layer. Changing the Blending Mode of the upper layer to **Difference** makes it easier to line them up perfectly.

Photoshop CS3 makes it even easier with its **Auto Align Layers** command (under the Edit menu). Of course if you use a tripod they should be pretty close to start with (I didn't in this case).

Now it's a simple case of adding a Layer Mask to the upper layer and painting with black to mask everything below the horizon.

Find Out More

Adjustment Layers: Page 44

Layer Masks: Page 38

Using Levels: Page 48

STUDIO FIX: PERFECT WHITE BACKGROUND

 10 MINUTES
 INTERMEDIATE

Getting a perfectly white background in-camera is difficult. Fortunately in Photoshop it's a breeze.

START HERE

 To complete this project you need basic Selection and Masking skills, plus an understanding of how Layers work.

 Also See:
Layer Basics: page 30
Layer Masks: page 38
The Magnetic Lasso: page 23
Modifying Selections: page 24

Whether you're shooting portraits in your home studio or simply trying to get more attractive images of your castoffs for selling on eBay, getting a true white background is a real challenge without extensive lighting setups. Here's how to use Photoshop to sort things out quickly.

Start Image

▲ This is a typical example of the kind of result you'll get using a cove or light tent. Without lighting the background, getting it perfectly white is nigh on impossible.

End Result

STEP 01

Start by opening your image in Photoshop and doing any basic colour corrections needed for the main subject.

STEP 02

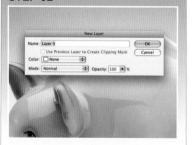

Turn the Background Layer into a normal, editable layer by double-clicking on it in the Layers palette and clicking OK when the **New Layer** dialog appears.

STEP 03

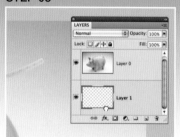

Create another new layer (**Layer>New>Layer** or Ctrl-Shift-N / ⌘-⇧-N). Drag the newly created empty layer to below the layer containing your image (Ctrl-[/ ⌘-[also moves a layer down the stack).

STEP 04

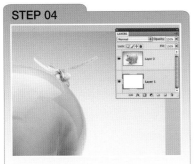

Fill the lower layer with white (the fastest way to do this is to press D to set the default Background Color to white, then Ctrl-Backspace / ⌘-⌫). Next click on the upper layer in the Layers palette to select it.

STEP 05

Now for the fiddly bit. You need to draw a selection around the subject. I'm using the **Magnetic Lasso** as the edge is fairly well defined. Don't worry about getting it perfect, we can fine-tune the selection in a moment.

STEP 06

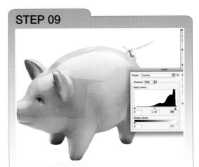

The Magnetic Lasso can produce slightly messy selections, so here I'm using Photoshop CS3's **Refine Edge** tool (see page 26) to smooth out the rough edges. If you're using an earlier version use **Select>Modify>Smooth**.

STEP 07

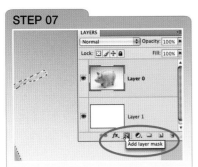

Once you're happy with your selection you need to add a Layer Mask to the upper layer. The quickest way is to click on the **Add Layer Mask** icon at the bottom of the Layers palette.

STEP 08

Zoom in and check the edges of your cut out. If it needs fine-tuning click on the Layer Mask and use a small brush with black paint to hide more of the original image and white paint to reveal more.

STEP 09

Now's a good time to sort out any brightness or contrast changes needed. Here, I'm using **Levels** on the upper layer (not the mask) to slightly brighten the pig.

STEP 10

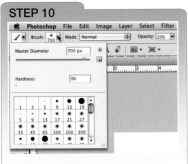

Lastly, we need to bring back the shadow under the pig. Select the **Brush** tool and choose a large, soft brush from the Options bar. Change the Opacity of the brush to around 20%.

STEP 11

Select the Layer Mask again and set the **Foreground Color** to white (press D then X). Carefully start to lay down brush strokes using white paint in the areas you want the shadow back.

Quick Tip

Creating a Shadow
Not happy with the existing shadow? After step 09 simply paint one on to the lower layer using the Brush tool and black paint at a low Opacity.

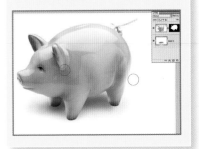

QUICK TECHNIQUE: ADDING A REFLECTION

You may have noticed that the Internet – and much of the rest of the world – seems to have gone shiny, with reflections appearing everywhere from adverts to web pages to the icons on your desktop. It's a great way to 'fancy up' dull product shots and to give your eBay pages a really professional look. Here's a quick step-by-step guide on how to create the effect yourself in Photoshop.

STEP 01

Start by duplicating the Background Layer. Create a selection around the object using any of the **Selection** tools.

STEP 02

Invert the selection (**Select>Inverse**) – so the background is selected – and press Delete.

STEP 03

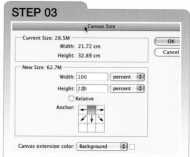

Use **Image>Canvas Size** to double the height of the canvas (using the top-middle Anchor point).

STEP 04

With the upper layer active, choose **Edit>Transform>Flip Vertical**.

STEP 05

Use the **Move** tool to reposition the flipped layer so the bottom edges of the two copies meet.

STEP 06

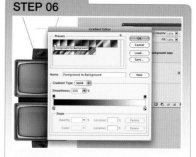

Select the **Gradient** tool and choose a black to white **Linear** gradient. Now add a Layer Mask to the upper layer.

STEP 07

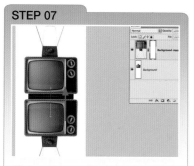

Click on the page about a third of the way up the copy layer and drag up to just beyond the join.

STEP 08

And that's it – you can now flatten the image and save it as a new file.

STEP 09

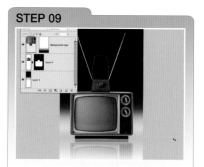

Now you can start to try different things such as changing the colour of the background.

CHAPTER SIX

PHOTO EFFECTS

For the creative photographer, the beauty of digital capture is how a single image can be the starting point for a thousand different treatments. From black and white to soft focus, to recreating the effect of specialist techniques such as fish-eye or infrared photography, Photoshop allows you to decide how you want your pictures to look after – not before – you take them.

This chapter looks at a range of simple Photoshop tools and techniques designed to recreate effects conventionally produced either at the time of shooting (by lens or film choice) or in the wet darkroom.

Some are designed to overcome the limitations imposed by shooting with digital cameras (compacts in particular), such as the inability to control depth of field, while others are designed to mimic the effect of techniques that are either difficult or impossible with consumer-level cameras.

As ever, we're only scratching the surface in these few pages, but the ideas and techniques described should give you a taste of just how easy it is to transform your images.

Finally in this chapter, you'll find some ideas for giving your photos a slightly less 'digital' feel, with retro-style colour effects, graininess and vignettes.

We'll be starting with the timeless appeal of black and white photography. Most cameras offer a black and white shooting mode, but Photoshop offers an almost limitless array of conversion options that allow you to tailor the black and white output in ways the traditional darkroom user could only dream of.

93

PHOTO EFFECTS:
CONVERTING TO BLACK AND WHITE

Photoshop boasts a variety of tools for creating black and white images from colour originals; some fully automatic, others offering full control over the process.

Of course, there was a time when there was *only* black and white; a time before photographs, magazines, newspapers, film and television burst into a world of colour. And over the past few years there has been a resurgence of interest in black and white for the enthusiast photographer looking to produce images with a certain 'something' that sets them apart from the crowd. Black and white photography is uniquely timeless; both cutting-edge and retro. Used skilfully it can even make a good picture truly great.

Photoshop Tools

Let's look at the six main methods on offer to Photoshop users wanting to turn a colour image to black and white and their relative benefits and drawbacks:

■ Grayscale Mode
Grayscale (Image>Mode>Grayscale) is a single channel mode that will turn your colour pictures monochrome with a single click. The results tend to look a little flat, but can usually be boosted with a little careful application of Curves or Levels. The main problem is the lack of control over how the different colours are represented, or how the individual channels of the image are blended.

Technique Tip: Quick Toning

To quickly create a toned mono image open Image>Adjustments>Hue/Saturation and click on the **Colorize** option.

Use the **Hue** and **Saturation** sliders to set the tone. Use a Hue/Saturation Adjustment Layer for non-permanent changes.

■ Lab Mode/Lightness Channel
Changing to Lab mode (Image>Mode>Lab Color) and discarding the **a** and **b** channels (leaving just the Lightness component) has two advantages. Firstly, it produces a result that often looks perfect without the need for more than a little tweaking of contrast. Secondly, as the Lightness channel rarely carries much noise, it can produce cleaner pictures.

■ Desaturate
Reducing the Saturation to zero (Image>Adjustments>Desaturate) produces a result very similar to Grayscale mode. Again, there's no control over how the various colours in the image are converted.

■ Gradient Map
Photoshop's Gradient Map (Image>Adjustments>Gradient Map), if used with a black to white gradient, can quickly produce a nice black and white image. By altering the ramp of the gradient you can tweak the distribution of tones, increase contrast or preserve fine highlight detail.

■ Channel Mixing
By far the most powerful and versatile option in Photoshop's arsenal of tools for making black and white photos, the Channel Mixer (Image>Adjustments>Channel Mixer) is also the most difficult to master. As its name implies, the Channel Mixer allows you to define what proportions of red, green and blue are used to make the final monochrome image. This allows more experienced users to recreate the effect of various different black and white emulsions as well as the

THE CHANNEL MIXER

Take control of your colour to black and white conversions.

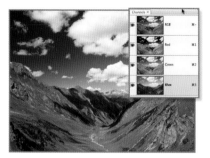

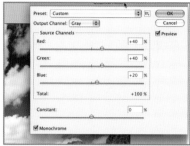

All full-colour images are made up of three (or more) grayscale channels – usually Red, Green and Blue. You can see them if you open the Channels palette (**Window>Channels**).

The Channel Mixer (**Image> Adjustments>Channel Mixer**) lets you decide how the three channels are blended – to make a black and white image check the **Monochrome** option.

Recent versions of Photoshop ship with a range of Channel Mixer Presets so you don't even need to change any settings yourself.

The key thing to remember with the Channel Mixer is that to retain the same brightness as the original, the three channels need to add up to 100%. Here's 100% Green.

By increasing the amount of Red you can reproduce the effect of an orange or yellow filter, which makes the blue sky get darker (above: 50% Red, 50% Green).

The Red channel on its own (100% Red, 0% Green and Blue) gives the effect of a red filter.

You need to experiment with different settings until you get the result you're looking for. Increasing the percentage makes those colours lighter, decreasing it makes them darker.

You can use negative numbers for any of the channels as long as you increase the others to compensate. Here's Red 164%, Green 25%, Blue -90%. The effect is a high-contrast, almost infrared style of image.

Quick Tips

■ If possible, use an Adjustment Layer (you can do this with all methods described here except converting to Grayscale mode) – this way you can go back and tweak the settings later if you need to. This also allows you to play with selective toning effects (see page 98).

■ Once you've converted to black and white, experiment with contrast adjustments using the tools covered on pages 48-58.

effect of using colour filters (such as a red filter for very dark skies).

■ Black & White Adjustment

New for Photoshop CS3 was the Black & White adjustment (**Image>Adjustments>Black & White**). The Black & White adjustment lets you choose how light or dark each of six colour groups (reds, greens, blues, yellows, cyans and magentas) will appear in the mono image using simple sliders ranging from 0% (very dark) to 300% (very pale). It also includes colour toning (something previously done using Hue/Saturation controls – see pages 61 and 94).

Black & White is also the first Photoshop adjustment to offer 'on image' adjustments (something there's a lot more of in version CS4). If you click anywhere on the image (with the Black & White dialog open) you can drag up and down to modify the slider that best matches the underlying colour. Thus darkening a blue sky is a simple matter of clicking on it and dragging to the left.

CHANNEL MIXING FOR SKIN TONES

Just as in conventional black and white photography, portraits require a different approach to that used for landscapes, so in Photoshop we tend to want to use different Channel Mixing settings for skin tones than we would for scenery (where we generally want blue skies to be dark and green foliage to be mid-grey).

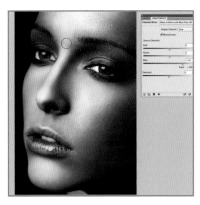

The Blue channel makes all warm tones in the image appear very dark.

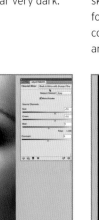

Increasing the amount of Red in the mix (here it's 50% Red, 50% Green and 0% Blue) produces paler skin tones and reduces the contrast between the skin and the red lips.

The Green channel renders Caucasian skin mid-grey and darkens the lips for better contrast. A green filter was commonly used in traditional black and white portraiture.

100% Red (and nothing else) produces very pale skin and lips. The only time you'd use this is if your subject has red skin blemishes (such as acne) which would disappear.

THE BLACK AND WHITE ADJUSTMENT (CS3)

Other B&W methods

Desaturating
Whether you use Image>Adjustment> Desaturate or the Saturation slider of the Hue/Saturation adjustment this is a quick way to take the colour out of an image.

The Black & White adjustment works in a slightly different way to the Channel Mixer. The six sliders adjust how the colours in the image will be rendered in the conversion, from dark (0%) to pale (300%). Thus you can choose to make skies very dark by simply moving the **Blues** slider to the left. Unlike the Channel Mixer you don't need to worry about getting everything to add up to 100%. Like the other adjustments there is also a range of useful Presets.

Grayscale Mode
Image>Mode>Grayscale discards all colours and produces a single channel image. Quick and easy, but tends to produce rather dull results.

Gradient Map
Image>Adjustments>Gradient Map is favoured by some photographers because it produces nice results for landscapes in a single click (using a black to white gradient).

▲ Click anywhere on the image to directly adjust the colours - click and drag to the left to darken and to the right to lighten the slider for the colours where you first clicked.

Editing the gradient gives you lots of control over how the image looks.

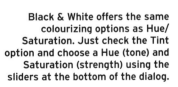

Black & White offers the same colourizing options as Hue/ Saturation. Just check the Tint option and choose a Hue (tone) and Saturation (strength) using the sliders at the bottom of the dialog.

SELECTIVE BLACK AND WHITE
🕐 10 MINUTES
📊 INTERMEDIATE

Draw attention to the main subject of your shot with this simple but very effective technique.

START HERE

Although this is a very simple technique it does require a little skill - specifically in making accurate selections. You'll also need a basic grasp of Adjustment Layers and Masks.

Also See:
Hue/Saturation: page 60
Adjustment Layers: page 44

There are many ways to add emphasis to part of a frame, and one of the most powerful is selective monochrome - turning an image to black and white but leaving a section in colour. Here's a simple technique using a Hue/Saturation Adjustment Layer.

Start Image

End Result

STEP 01

Start by opening your image and creating a selection around the area you want to keep coloured. In this case I'm using the **Magnetic Lasso** as the edge of the flower is sharp and fairly well defined. You can of course create the selection using whichever of the Selection tools are best suited to the image you're actually working on.

STEP 02

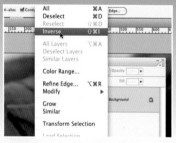

Choose **Select>Inverse** (to invert the selection so everything but the flower is selected). Now create a new Hue/Saturation Adjustment Layer using the **Layer>New Adjustment Layer** menu. Of course you can use whichever adjustment you prefer for the black and white conversion - this is simply a quick example.

STEP 03

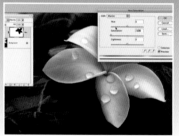

When the **Hue/Saturation** dialog appears simply reduce the Saturation slider to -100. You can now zoom in and check the edge of the coloured section is perfect; if not simply edit the Adjustment Layer's mask with the **Brush** tool as usual (see page 45).

SELECTIVE TONING TIPS

You don't always need to start with a selection – for a really quick result just paint on to a mask.

▲ Use a duplicate layer converted to black and white and add a mask. You can now quickly paint on to the mask with a large, soft brush to reveal the colour version underneath. Remember, black on the mask will hide the black and white version and let the colour through.

▲ Of course, you don't need to create a sharp transition between the colour and black and white areas of the frame, nor do you need to restrict it to one particular element in the image. Here, I've spent a few minutes playing around with a masked black and white duplicate layer. Using the Brush tool at less than 100% Opacity allowed me to create areas where the black and white layer is semi-transparent (giving a low saturation, rather than a purely monochrome result).

Technique Tip: History Brush

Here's another alternative technique that's very quick. Start by converting the image to black and white using Image>Adjustments> Black & White (though it doesn't matter which tool you use – except converting to Grayscale mode, which won't work).

Open the **History** palette (Window>History) and click in the little box to the left of the History step before you did the black and white conversion (in this case it's the Open step, since the Black & White adjustment was the first thing I did after opening the file).

Now choose the **History Brush** tool (keyboard shortcut: Y) and try painting on to the image. What you're doing is effectively painting with an Undo brush, taking the image back to how it was before you converted to black and white (in other words, back to colour).

In this case, bringing back the colour in the owl's eyes took a matter of seconds (using a large, soft brush). If you make a mistake simply change the History Brush source to the Black & White step (see above) and paint over your edits.

SOFTENING AND DIFFUSING EFFECTS
 5 MINUTES
EASY

START HERE

 This is a deceptively simple technique that - if you experiment with different Blending Modes - can produce a myriad of different results from the same two-layer sandwich.

 Also See:
Layer Blending Modes: page 32
Layer Masks: page 39

This is a simple layering technique that can produce an amazing variety of results in a matter of seconds.

Not everything in digital imaging is about getting the sharpest possible result; sometimes you want something a little softer – particularly when you're dealing with portraits.

In the days before digital getting a soft-focus effect for portraits meant using special filters (or a pair of tights) in front of the lens and careful aperture control to get the right effect. These days soft focus is only a click away, and the variety of effects you can get is almost limitless. This section looks at how to create soft-focus effects (which aren't simple blurs) using layers.

Although any portrait can have the soft-focus effect applied it works better with some than others (most grown men, for example, don't really want to see themselves photographed with a soft-focus effect). Ideally you want a good sharp starting image.

STEP 01

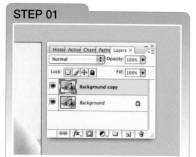

To create a simple soft-focus effect open your image and duplicate the Background Layer (Ctrl-J / ⌘-J) so you've got two copies of the image in separate layers.

STEP 02

Run the **Gaussian Blur** filter (**Filter> Gaussian Blur**) on the top (duplicate) layer. The settings will vary according to the size of the image and the amount of softness you want. A 4-6-pixel Radius is usually best.

STEP 03

To get the diffused soft-focus effect you simply need to reduce the Opacity of the blurred layer. Experiment a little, but you'll probably find that a figure between about 60 and 75% gives the nicest result.

VARIATIONS ON THE TECHNIQUE

Once you've started experimenting with blurred duplicate layers you'll soon discover that the creative possibilities are endless.

The **Blending Mode** of the upper (blurred) layer has a huge effect on how the image looks (see below). Try changing to **Screen** mode for a more high-key effect.

You'll probably want to change the upper layer's Opacity back to 100% as the effect in Screen mode is subtler.

Smart Filters (CS2+)
Turning the Background Layer into a **Smart Object** (see pages 36 and 81) allows you to do everything on these pages with a single layer. Run the **Gaussian Blur** filter on the Smart Object and you can go back and change the Blending Mode and Opacity of the filter as many times as you wish – as well as masking it to restrict the blurring effect to specific areas of the frame.

Try masking the blurred layer in the area around the eyes and the centre of the face. This allows the sharp original to show through in these areas only, giving a soft-focus vignette effect.

Changing the Blending Mode of the upper layer to **Multiply** causes the shadows to bleed into the highlights. The result is much better suited to this atmospheric shot.

Multiply also intensifies colours. For a subtler effect, try desaturating the blurred layer by reducing the Saturation to zero.

Here's another variation; the upper layer has been desaturated and the Blending Mode changed to **Overlay**. The result is an increase in contrast and very subtle softening.

SOFTENING BLACK AND WHITE IMAGES

Using a blurred duplicate layer with different Blending Modes is a technique that works particularly well with black and white images. Take some time out to experiment with all the different blending, transparency and toning options and you'll soon discover that you can produce hundreds of different results from a single image with very little effort involved. Because you don't need to worry about colour shifts you can actually take black and white shots a lot further, using more than one duplicate layer to build up effects and masking the areas you want to keep sharp.

▲ Start by converting your image to black and white using one of the methods discussed on pages 94-97.

▲ Using a blurred duplicate layer in Overlay mode produces a slightly spooky high-contrast effect.

In this example the blurred layer was set to **Multiply** mode (which causes the shadows to bleed into the highlights) and the eye area was masked to keep it sharp.

And here's the same image as shown on the left after the contrast has been increased using **Curves**. The beauty of black and white is that it is considerably more malleable than colour when experimenting with this kind of technique.

Colourizing the upper layer (using **Image>Adjustments>Hue/ Saturation**) allows you to tone the image at the same time as adding the softening or diffusing effect. Note that if your image is in Grayscale mode you'll need to covert back to RGB mode (**Image>Mode>RGB**) first.

USING BLUR: DEPTH OF FIELD EFFECT 1
🕐 15 MINUTES
▦ EASY

This technique recreates the effect of a very narrow depth of field for portraits using localized blurring.

START HERE

 This technique is surprisingly easy and doesn't take long to master. You'll need to be able to create and edit Layers and Layer Masks and use the Brush tool.

 Also See:
Layer Masks: page 39
Black and White: page 94
Sharpening: page 64

Unless you've got a digital SLR with an expensive prime lens, getting very narrow depth of field is virtually impossible. This project shows you how to recreate the effect of this selective focus technique using Photoshop's blurring and masking tools. The result may not be perfect but it doesn't take long and is a great way to get rid of cluttered backgrounds in portraits.

Start Image

Start with a good, sharp portrait. This effect can be applied to virtually any portrait but is easiest with those taken face on, i.e. with the sitter looking straight at the camera.

End Result

STEP 01

Create a duplicate of the Background Layer (**Layer>Duplicate** or Ctrl-J / ⌘-J). Now add a Layer Mask (**Layer>Layer Mask>Reveal All**) to the new layer (we'll use this later to restrict the areas where the blurring is applied).

STEP 02

Making sure you've got the upper layer selected, (not its mask), choose the **Gaussian Blur** filter, (**Filter>Blur>Gaussian Blur**). The Radius setting used will depend on the size of your image, but start with something around 6 or 7 pixels. You want it to look out of focus, not totally blurred away.

STEP 03

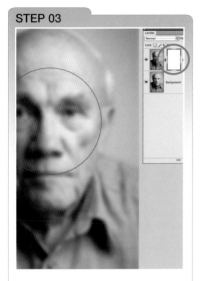

Now click on the mask icon for the upper layer, (the white icon on the Layers palette). Select a large, soft brush and use black paint on the mask to reveal any areas you want to be sharp, starting in the middle of the face.

STEP 04

Use a smaller brush (with hardness set to zero) to fine-tune the mask until you're happy that the front of the face is sharp and gets gradually softer in areas that are further away from the lens. Use black on the mask to hide the blurred layer, white to reveal it.

STEP 05

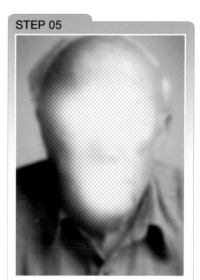

Here's the upper layer after I'd finished tweaking its mask (I temporarily hid the Background Layer before taking this screenshot). As you can see I've tried to create a single plane of focus around the eyes and mouth. The mask has a very soft edge.

LENS BLUR

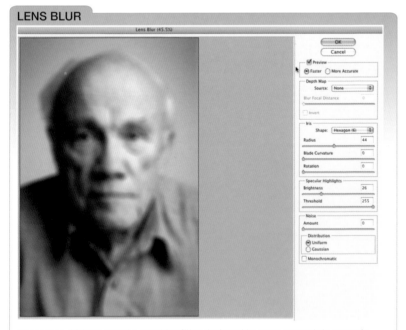

Photoshop CS introduced a new blur filter designed to more accurately recreate the out of focus effect, **Lens Blur (Filter>Blur>Lens Blur)**. It does produce more realistic results, especially if you set the **Depth Map Source** to **Mask**. If you're using CS2 or later combine this with a **Smart Layer** for total control.

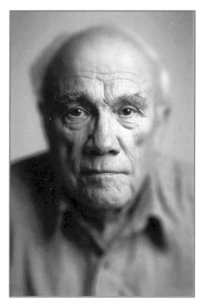

Some final finishing touches could include sharpening the lower (non-blurred) layer a little, flattening the image, converting to Grayscale mode and increasing the contrast slightly.

USING BLUR: DEPTH OF FIELD EFFECT 2
 20 MINUTES
ADVANCED

Isolate your subject from a messy background with this 'fast telephoto' depth of field effect.

START HERE

 As with all localized filtering effects this all comes down to how accurately you can make selections. The technique described requires the Lens Blur filter, so won't work with Photoshop 7.0 (see page 107).

 Also See:
The Magnetic Lasso: page 23
Quick Mask mode: page 27

End Result

Start Image

Professional photographers use fast (wide aperture) long telephoto lenses to isolate subjects from cluttered backgrounds using narrow depth of field. Digital compact cameras and digital SLR kit zooms make this technique difficult, if not impossible. In this variation of the previous technique we're going to recreate the isolating effect of narrow depth of field telephoto shots using Photoshop's Lens Blur filter (**Filter>Blur>Lens Blur...**).

STEP 01

The key to success is to create an accurate selection around the main subject. I've used the **Magnetic Lasso**, which works well with clean edges.

STEP 02

Create the best selection you can with your preferred tool. Zoom in and have a look at the selection – in this case I can see that the Magnetic Lasso has made a few mistakes so I want to fine-tune the selection.

STEP 03

Press Q to enter Quick Mask mode and select the **Brush** tool (press B). Work your way around the image using the brush to get the Quick Mask to fit the edge of your subject perfectly.

STEP 04

Use black to add to the mask (remove areas from the selection) and white to add to the selection. For the really fiddly areas you'll need to use a very small brush with a high Hardness (you don't want a soft-edged selection).

STEP 05

Once you're happy that the selection is perfect press Q again to exit Quick Mask mode.

STEP 06

Choose **Select>Inverse** (so the background you want to blur is now selected). Then choose **Filter>Blur>Lens Blur....**

STEP 07

When the **Lens Blur** dialog appears the only thing you need to change is the **Radius** slider (as this defines the amount of blurring), but feel free to experiment with all the options. When you're happy, press OK and wait.

Quick Tip: Using a Mask

If you want to work in a non-destructive manner with the Lens Blur filter, you need to work in a slightly different way to normal, filtering the masked layer, not the underlying layer (as might seem the obvious thing to do):

■ Start by duplicating the Background Layer and creating the selection (on the upper layer) in the same way as steps 01–05.

■ With the upper layer selected and your selection active choose **Layer>Layer Mask>Hide Selection**.

■ Now run the Lens Blur filter on the upper layer, making sure you choose

Mask from the Depth Map **Source** menu. You can now fine-tune the mask to ensure the edge is perfect.

■ If you try to blur the Background Layer and place the masked, sharp layer on top, you'll be able to see the edges of the blurred version of your sharp subject spreading out into the background (see opposite).

QUICK TECHNIQUE: GRADUATED MASK

Sometimes you don't need to make a selection or even paint the mask to get a narrow depth of field effect; all you need is Quick Mask and the Gradient tool.

Images such as this work well for this simple effect; the contents of the frame clearly get further away from left to right.

Pop into **Edit in Quick Mask Mode** and draw a gradient from black to white on the Quick Mask using the **Gradient** tool (just click and drag).

Press Q to turn the Quick Mask back into a selection and run the Lens Blur filter. The result is a perfectly convincing depth of field effect in a few clicks.

PHOTOSHOP 7.0 TECHNIQUE

Unfortunately the Lens Blur filter wasn't introduced until Photoshop CS, which means you have to work around the limitations of the Gaussian Blur filter.

▲ One solution is to make the upper layer bigger using **Edit>Transform>Scale**, but this won't work for a complex subject like this.

▼ Often the easiest way to get around the problem is to paste the cut out subject (as a new layer) on to a new background with similar colours, which is what was done here.

▲ Creating a selection around the main subject, inverting (so the background is selected) then running the **Gaussian Blur** filter clearly shows the problem: a ghostly halo around the subject (where the edge of the main subject has blurred into the background). This is not exactly what we were looking for.

CROSS-PROCESS EFFECT

10 MINUTES
INTERMEDIATE

There are many ways to create the popular cross-process effect; here's just one of them.

START HERE

This technique works with any version of Photoshop and makes use of Layers, Color Modes, Levels and the Gaussian Blur filter.

Also See:
Layers: page 30
Levels and Histograms: page 48
Curves: page 54

End Result

Cross-process effects are notoriously difficult to reproduce in software.

Start Image

STEP 01

Open your image and - if necessary - tweak the contrast and saturation to give a nice vivid look. Change the colour mode to Lab (**Image>Mode>Lab Color**). Duplicate the Background Layer.

STEP 02

With the new (duplicate) layer selected, open the **Channels** palette and click on the **a** channel. Choose **Filter>Blur>Gaussian Blur** and set the Radius to around 7 or 8 pixels. Click on OK. Go back to the Channels palette and click on the top thumbnail (Lab) to reveal all channels.

STEP 03

With the upper layer still selected, Choose **Image>Adjustments>Levels**. Choose **a** from the Channel menu at the top of the Levels dialog. Set the **Input Levels** to roughly 80, 1.0, 255 and leave the **Output Levels** untouched.

STEP 04

Now select the **b** channel from the menu at the top of the Levels dialog. This time set the Input Levels to 75, 1.5, 255 and click OK. Note that there's considerable room for experimentation with Levels in both this step and the previous one.

STEP 05

Change the Blending Mode of the upper layer to **Overlay** or **Vivid Light**. Experiment with altering the contrast (using Curves) or colour (using Hue/Saturation) of both layers until you get a result you like. When you're happy, convert back to **RGB mode**.

FAKE INFRARED EFFECT

🕐 10 MINUTES
📊 INTERMEDIATE

Infrared photography is difficult to get right and needs special equipment. Here's a technique for faking it.

START HERE

⚙ Like that on the opposite page, this technique looks complicated because it involves running filters on individual colour channels. It is, in fact, very straightforward and as long as you follow the steps carefully it shouldn't take more than a few minutes.

🔍 **Also See:**
Channel Mixer: page 95

End Result

Start Image

STEP 01

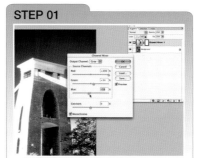

Open the image and perform any necessary colour, brightness, contrast and sharpness corrections. Add a Channel Mixer Adjustment Layer (**Layer>New Adjustment Layer>Channel Mixer...**). Set the sliders as follows; Red +200%; Green +34%; Blue - (minus) 18 or 20%. Tick the **Monochrome** option.

STEP 02

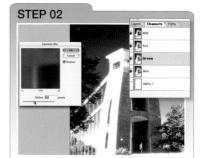

Select the Background Layer, go to the **Channels** palette and click on the Green channel. Run the Gaussian Blur filter (**Filter>Blur>Gaussian Blur**) at a Radius of around 8 or 9 pixels on the Green channel.

STEP 03

Choose **Edit>Fade Gaussian Blur...** and change the Mode to **Screen** and the Opacity to about 70% - use the on-screen preview to decide what setting works best. Click on the RGB channel again to make all channels visible.

STEP 04

Now to go back to the Background Layer and add some noise – infrared pictures tend to be very grainy. Choose **Filter>Noise>Add Noise** and set the amount fairly low – maybe 10 or 12% at the most - and use the **Gaussian** and **Monochromatic** options.

STEP 05

Finally, tweak the Levels on the Background Layer as necessary to get the right contrast.

GRITTY AND GRAINY MOVIE EFFECT

 10 MINUTES

 EASY

Give your images a gritty, grainy retro feel
that's more than a little 'film noir'.

START HERE

You'll need a basic grasp of Selection and tonal correction tools for this project. The method is the same for all versions of Photoshop.

Also See:
Levels and Histograms: page 48
Curves: page 54
Hue/Saturation: page 60
Selection tools: page 20

Start Image

As with most post-processing the key to success with a technique like this is the choice of image. The 'grungy' effect doesn't suit bright sunny day pictures of happy people, but is great for low-light shots in urban settings.

End Result

STEP 01

Start by really pushing the contrast up using **Image>Adjustments>Curves** and a fairly steep 'S' shaped curve.

STEP 02

Now open the **Hue/Saturation** controls (**Image>Adjustments>Hue/Saturation**) and reduce the Saturation significantly. You want only a hint of the original colour (around -60 to -70 should suffice).

STEP 03

Now to add some grainy noise. There are several ways to add noise to an image, for this example I'm using the **Grain** filter (**Filter>Texture>Grain...**). Use the **Enlarged** Grain Type.

STEP 04

You don't want the colour in the grain so choose **Edit>Fade Grain**. When the **Fade** dialog appears change the Mode to **Luminosity**.

STEP 05

I'm just tweaking the contrast using **Levels** (**Image>Adjustments>Levels**) at this point - you may not need to.

STEP 06

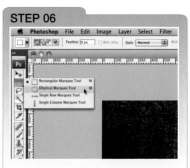

As a finishing touch add some corner shading; this effect is a little over-used but does add an authentic retro feel. Select the **Elliptical Marquee** tool.

STEP 07

Use the Elliptical Marquee tool to draw a large oval like the one shown above. Use the **Select>Transform Selection** command to resize it if you can't get it right first time.

STEP 08

Feather the selection by around 60 pixels (**Select>Modify>Feather** or **Select>Feather** in older versions of Photoshop). Click OK and then invert the selection (**Select>Inverse**).

Quick Tip

Lens Correction (CS2+)
If you're using a later version of Photoshop you can cut steps 06-10 out by using the **Vignette** control slider in the **Lens Correction** filter. (**Filter>Distort>Lens Correction**).

STEP 09

Open the **Brightness/Contrast** dialog (**Image>Adjustments>Brightness/ Contrast**). If you're using Photoshop CS3 check the **Use Legacy** option.

STEP 10

Reduce the **Brightness** slider to around -60 or until you're happy with the effect.

Shortcuts

Marquee   [M]
(⇧ – M to cycle tools)

Fade (last filter)   ⌘ ⇧ / Ctrl ⇧ – [F]

Levels   ⌘ / Ctrl – [L]

Curves   ⌘ / Ctrl – [M]   **Hue/Saturation**   ⌘ / Ctrl – [U]

Invert Selection   ⌘ alt / Ctrl alt – [I]   **Feather Selection**   ⌘ alt / Ctrl alt – [D]

VINTAGE EFFECT: RETRO FADED PRINT

10 MINUTES
INTERMEDIATE

This technique uses Curves to create a retro colour effect, reminiscent of vintage prints.

START HERE

The main part of this technique uses only two tools: Curves and the Hue/Saturation controls. The Lens Correction filter isn't available in version CS or earlier.

Also See:
Curves: page 54
Gritty and Grainy Movie Effect: page 110
Cross-Process Effect: page 108

End Result

Start Image

This retro-themed step-by-step project puts to use the power of Curves to subtly alter the balance of the individual colour channels in the image. The result is a vintage look that gives a fairly close approximation of the way the dyes in photographic prints from the '50s, '60s and '70s look after decades of fading. Although

you can use this technique on any image it works best on shots with a somewhat timeless look to them, and tends to produce the strongest results when there's lots of not-too-deep blue sky in the shot. You will need to tweak the settings used in the following steps according to the image you're working on.

STEP 01

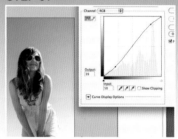

Start by increasing the contrast of the image slightly (unless it's already very contrasty). You can use the standard Brightness/Contrast tools if you prefer, but I'm going to use **Curves** and a gentle 'S' curve. Click OK to accept the changes.

STEP 02

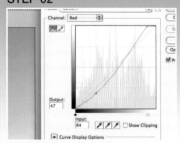

Now to get to work on the colour. If it is not already active from step 01, open the **Curves** palette (**Image> Adjustments>Curves**). From the **Channel** drop-down menu choose the **Red** channel. Change the shape of the red curve roughly to match what is shown here.

STEP 03

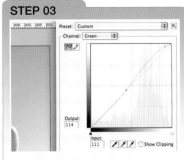

Now choose the **Green** channel from the drop-down menu and change the shape of the green curve to approximate the one shown here.

STEP 04

Switch to the **Blue** channel and reduce the angle of the curve as shown here (the more you move the end points along each axis the stronger the effect becomes). Click OK to accept the changes.

STEP 05

Finally experiment with different Saturation levels (using **Image>Adjustments>Hue/ Saturation**). Most images will look more retro if you reduce the Saturation (as here).

STEP 06

To finish off the effect, add a vintage-style vignette. If you're using Photoshop CS2 or later choose **Filter>Distort>Lens Correction** (for older versions use the technique described on page 111).

STEP 07

In the **Vignette** section, move the **Amount** slider to around -50 and the **Midpoint** slider to around +60 (take these as a starting point; the exact values are up to you).

Technique Tip

Quick Antique Print Effect
Sometimes you want to take an image more than a few decades back – for a really vintage antique effect you'll need a slightly different technique.

▲ First **Colorize** the image using the Hue/Saturation controls (set the Hue to around 33 for a sepia effect).

▲ Use **Filter>Texture>Grain** and the **Vertical** Grain Type for a grungy, dirty old print effect.

Finally, reduce the contrast (using **Brightness/ Contrast**) and add a vignette as shown on this page or using the technique on page 111.

Quick Tips

■ If you find a setting you particularly like Photoshop allows you to save it as a Curves Preset.

■ Try shooting images specifically designed for use with this technique. Shots of classic cars and buildings from the '50s to '70s also respond well to this kind of treatment.

■ If you want to experiment with different Curves use an Adjustment Layer for steps 02–04.

FAKE FISH-EYE EFFECT
 10 MINUTES
INTERMEDIATE

The effect produced by a fish-eye lens is unmistakable; here's how to fake it in Photoshop.

 START HERE

This is a simple technique that makes use of Photoshop's venerable Distortion filter. It works best with landscape images. Remember that you can apply the filter more than once for a stronger effect.

 Also See:
Fake Miniature Model Effect: page 134

End Result

The best photos for this effect are those taken with a wide lens, and one where the main subject isn't too close to the edge.

Start Image

STEP 01

If your photo needs any colour or contrast adjustments do them now. Choose **Image>Image Size...** from the Image menu (or press Ctrl-Alt-i / ⌘-⌥-i). Uncheck the **Constrain Proportions** option, and change the width figure to match the height figure. Click OK – your picture should now be a square.

STEP 02

Choose **Filter>Distort>Spherize**. When the dialog box shown here appears move the slider to 100%, and leave the Mode set to **Normal**. Now, select the **Elliptical Marquee** tool. Hold down the Shift key and click and drag across the image to create a perfect circular selection to match the distorted area.

STEP 03

If you can't create a selection that matches the circle exactly, choose **Select>Transform Selection** and – holding down the Shift key to keep the shape a perfect circle – drag the corner handles to scale the selection.

STEP 04

Invert the selection (**Select>Inverse**) and choose **Edit>Fill**. When the Fill dialog appears choose **Black** from the **Use** menu. Click OK.

STEP 05

For a finishing touch, invert the selection again and choose **Filter> Render>Lens Flare**. Click on the preview in the Lens Flare dialog and place the **Flare Center** on the edge of the circle – at around the 2 o'clock position.

CHAPTER SEVEN

ART AND SPECIAL EFFECTS

Photoshop's ability to radically transform images from photographs into anything from bold Warhol-style graphics to watercolour paintings, makes it a powerful tool for the digital artist. This chapter gives you just a taste of some of the dramatic effects you can achieve with relatively simple techniques.

Of course, technically Photoshop can't do any of these things; that's down to you. Anyone expecting to be able to produce amazing works of art with a single click is going to be very disappointed.

Sure, Photoshop has a lot of art filters designed to mimic real-world painting and sketching techniques, but the results are rarely that impressive (if you want highly realistic natural-media effects take a look at Corel Painter).

Not only are they not terribly convincing, they are instantly recognizable as being produced by Photoshop's built-in effects. Too many novice users make the

mistake of thinking a poor or just plain old boring photograph will suddenly become a work of art just because they've run the Find Edges filter on it.

I should also make a confession here; personally speaking I just don't like digital paint effects. It does nothing for me to see a photograph turned into an oil painting, no matter how convincingly. I guess I like photographs to be photographs and paintings to be produced directly on paper. So I make no apologies for the fact that this section only briefly touches on techniques for recreating natural media techniques.

QUICK GRAPHIC LAYERING EFFECTS

 5 MINUTES
 EASY

Totally transform your photos into dramatic high-contrast graphics in a couple of simple steps.

START HERE

 Photoshop offers so many ways to produce bold, graphic effects – from simply whacking up the contrast or saturation to clever layer blending techniques – that the best advice I can give is simply to experiment.

Also See:
Create a Fake Andy Warhol: page 120
Layer Blending Modes: page 32

On page 43 we saw how using Layer Blending Modes to mix an image with an altered version of itself can dramatically transform it, and on pages 100–102 we used a similar technique to produce a variety of softening effects.

Over the next few pages we're going to be looking at some very easy two- or three-step techniques for quickly producing bold, graphic images from your photos. Take the ideas here as a starting point; even the smallest change in the settings used will often produce radically different results, and the key thing, as ever, is to experiment. Keep notes of what you do so you can repeat the process if you hit on an effect you really like.

STEP 01

We'll start with the poster effect shown on the left. Open your image and duplicate the Background Layer (press Ctrl-J / ⌘-J).

STEP 02

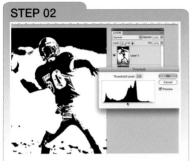

With the upper layer active choose **Image>Adjustments>Threshold** and move the slider until you're happy with the black/white balance. You can also try **Filter>Sketch>Stamp** or **Filter>Sketch>Torn Edges** for a different effect.

STEP 03

Change the Blending Mode of the upper layer to **Multiply** or **Darken**. Select the lower layer and increase the Saturation considerably using **Image>Adjustments>Hue/Saturation**. That's all there is to it.

STEP 04

For a slightly different effect try colourizing the lower layer (again using the **Hue/Saturation** controls – see pages 61 and 94).

TRY THIS: MAKE ANYONE INTO A CARTOON

Use this variation of the previous technique to produce your very own old-school cartoon.

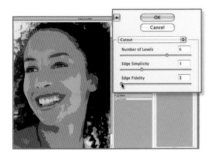

Duplicate the Background Layer, but this time run the **Halftone Pattern** filter on the upper layer (found under the **Filter>Sketch** menu). Use the settings shown as a starting point.

Go back to the Background Layer and choose **Filter>Artistic>Cutout**. Move the sliders until you get the right balance of tone and detail.

Finally change the Blending Mode of the upper layer to **Soft Light** and increase the Saturation of the bottom layer. For this example, I also painted with solid colour on to the bottom layer to bring a little more colour into the white areas of the frame.

OTHER QUICK LAYERING IDEAS

Start experimenting with layering for graphic effect and you'll soon discover that there's no limit to the results you can get in one or two simple steps.

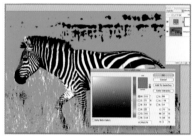

Using the same technique as described on page 117 with the Background Layer posterized (Image> Adjustments>Posterize) to 4 levels for a more graphic colour effect.

Here's the same technique again – the only difference this time is that the Background Layer has been blurred using Filter>Artistic>Paint Daubs.

Here's a very quick technique for radical graphic effects. Rather than duplicating the Background Layer, add a **Solid Color Fill Layer** (Layer>New Fill Layer>Solid Color) – pick any colour then change its Blending Mode to **Hard Mix**. Now experiment with different colours for the Fill Layer by double-clicking on its thumbnail.

PSEUDO-SOLARIZATION

Solarization has been a popular – if difficult to control – darkroom effect since it was first discovered in the 19th century, and has long been associated with the photographer who made it famous: Man Ray.

STEP 01

Start by desaturating the image (Image>Adjustments>Desaturate) then bring up the **Curves** dialog (Image>Adjustments>Curves). Pull both ends of the curve to the top and pull down the middle to create this 'V' shaped curve.

STEP 02

I always think a solarized image looks better with a subtle tone – here I'm using the **Color Balance** controls (Image>Adjustments>Color Balance) to add a cool blue hue.

TRY THIS: URBAN COLOUR EFFECT

STEP 01

You don't always need to turn everything up to get a bold graphic effect; sometimes subtlety is called for. Start by opening your image and fixing any exposure problems using **Levels** (see page 49).

STEP 02

Use a Hue/Saturation Adjustment Layer to reduce the overall Saturation to about -70. In this case I also selected **Greens** from the edit menu and reduced their Saturation to -100.

STEP 03

Go back to the Background Layer and choose **Filter>Sharpen>Unsharp Mask**. Use a large Radius (80-120 pixels) and an Amount of around 75-100%.

STEP 04

For an optional finishing touch use a **Color Balance Adjustment Layer** to add a yellowish tinge to the mid-tones (a setting of +24, +7, -37 was used here).

MORE SIMPLE GRAPHIC EFFECTS

An entire book could be filled with the ways Photoshop offers to give your photos a bold, graphic makeover.

Use Levels or Curves to massively increase contrast, then Colorize.

Use Hard Mix to blend a heavily blurred duplicate Layer.

Add a multicoloured Gradient Map Adjustment Layer.

CREATE A FAKE ANDY WARHOL
 30 MINUTES
 ADVANCED

For a truly eye-catching graphic effect take a cue from of one of the 20th century's most iconic artists.

START HERE

 You'll need a basic understanding of Layer, Selection and Paint tools, but if you follow the steps below carefully you shouldn't have any serious problems.

Also See:
Graphic Layering Effects: page 116
Layers: page 30
Hue/Saturation: page 60
Levels and Histograms: page 48

End Result

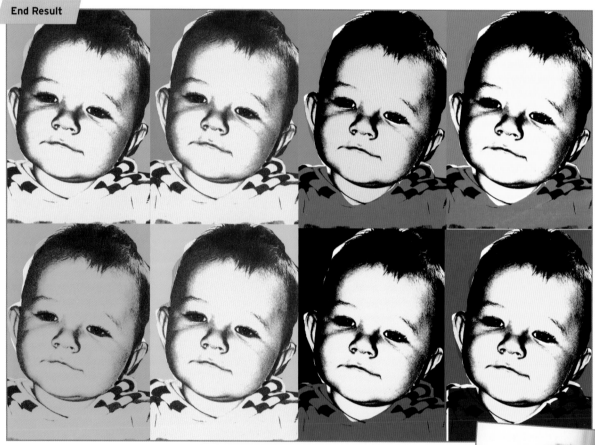

Start Image

Andy Warhol produced some of the most striking images of the Pop Art era, and half a century later his unmistakable silk-screen portraits sell for millions. Turning one of your own snaps into a fake Warhol is pretty simple, and the result is a graphic portrait that will add a bold touch to any living room ... and it's a lot cheaper than buying a real one!

To produce our fake Warhol we're going to use a variation of the layering technique discussed on pages 116 and 117, and although the process is quite long-winded, it's also very simple and shouldn't take too long to master.

STEP 01

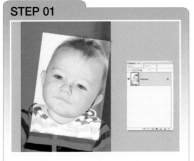

Start with a good, sharp portrait; flash shots with plenty of contrast seem best. Crop the image (here I'm also rotating the image to straighten up the face).

STEP 02

Increase the contrast slightly – here I'm using **Levels** but you can use any of the contrast tools (Brightness/Contrast, Levels, Curves, Shadow/Highlight etc.).

STEP 03

Use the **Lasso** (the freehand Selection tool) to draw around the entire head roughly – don't worry about it being too accurate (the effect won't work if you make a perfect selection around the head), but try not to take the selection into the face if possible.

STEP 04

We want to put the cut-out head into a new layer; you can do this directly using the **Layer>New>Layer Via Copy** menu.

STEP 05

Go back to the Background Layer (click on it in the Layers palette) and delete its contents (**Edit>Select All**, then press Backspace).

STEP 06

Now fill the Background Layer with a bright colour; here I'm using a rather unpleasant luminous green, but it really doesn't matter what colour you use (we'll be changing it later).

STEP 07

The easiest way to fill is with the **Paint Bucket** tool. We've now finished with the background for a while, so click on the top layer to select it.

STEP 08

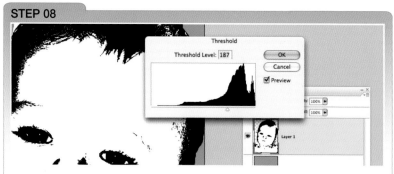

This step – turning the portrait into a graphic black and white 'screen print' – is a key one, and there are several ways to do it. One is to use the **Threshold** command (**Image>Adjustments>Threshold…**), which turns every pixel either black or white (the slider defines where the black/white split occurs in the tonal range). Move the slider left and right until you get the right balance of detail.

STEP 09

Later versions of Photoshop have a much better option. Start by removing the colour from the top layer by reducing the Saturation to -100 (**Image>Adjustments>Hue/Saturation**).

STEP 10

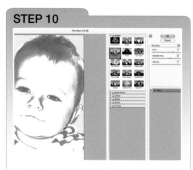

Choose **Filter>Artistic>Film Grain**. Start with a high **Intensity** level (10), and a fairly high **Grain** level (12-18), then adjust the **Highlight Area** until the majority of the skin areas are white, as here. Click OK.

STEP 11

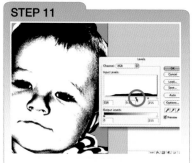

We need one more step to get the perfect effect. Choose **Image>Adjustments>Levels** and drag the black (left) slider over to just beyond the half-way point to get the high-contrast effect we're after.

STEP 12

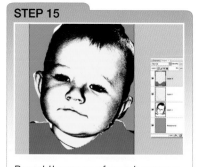

Now to start adding the Warhol colour. Create a new empty (transparent) layer and – using the Lasso tool – draw a rough selection around the area you want to colour in (here I've selected the face, ears and neck, roughly).

STEP 13

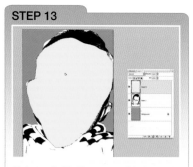

Pick a suitable Foreground Color and use the **Paint Bucket** tool to fill the selection made in step 12.

STEP 14

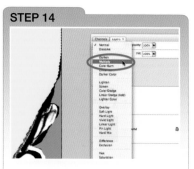

Change the Blending Mode of the layer created in step 12 and 13 (the coloured shape) to **Multiply** and reduce its Opacity to around 80%.

STEP 15

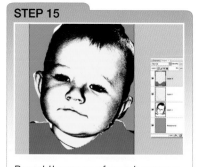

Repeat the process for each area you want to colour (note also that I've erased rough 'holes' in the yellow/skin layer for the whites of the eyes).

STEP 16

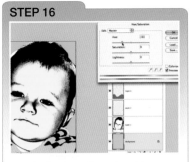

Now to fine-tune the colour. Use **Image>Adjustments>Hue/Saturation** to alter the colour (Hue), strength (Saturation) and Lightness of each of the colour layers until you're happy with the result.

STEP 17

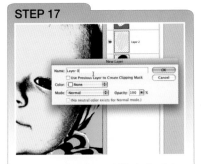

The other signature of Warhol's style was repetition - more specifically repetition with variation. Start by double-clicking the Background Layer to make it editable (just click OK when the **New Layer** dialog appears).

STEP 18

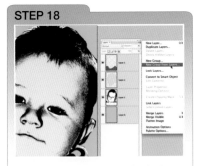

Select all the layers by Shift-clicking on them in the Layers palette and choose **Layer>Group Layers** (or choose **New Group From Layers** from the Layers palette flyout menu.

STEP 19

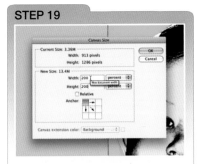

Choose **Image>Canvas Size** and double the width and height of the Canvas using one of the corners as the Anchor.

STEP 20

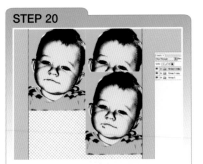

You can now duplicate the Group three times either using the Menu (**Layer>Duplicate Group**) or by holding down the Alt (⌥) key as you drag the Group using the **Move** tool.

STEP 21

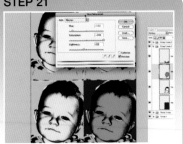

Use the **Hue/Saturation** controls on each of the colour layers to create interesting variations.

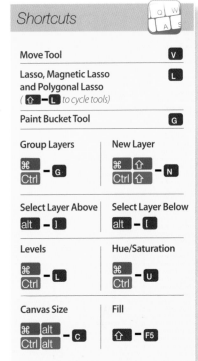

Shortcuts

Move Tool	**V**
Lasso, Magnetic Lasso and Polygonal Lasso (⇧ – **L** to cycle tools)	**L**
Paint Bucket Tool	**G**

Group Layers	New Layer
⌘ – **G** / Ctrl	⌘ ⇧ – **N** / Ctrl ⇧

Select Layer Above	Select Layer Below
alt – **]**	alt – **[**

Levels	Hue/Saturation
⌘ – **L** / Ctrl	⌘ – **U** / Ctrl

Canvas Size	Fill
⌘ alt – **C** / Ctrl alt	⇧ – **F5**

Quick Tips

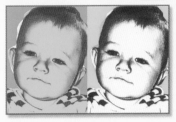

■ As a variation try changing the colour of the portrait layer from black to a different colour (using the Hue/Saturation **Colorize** option).

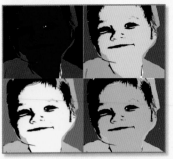

■ Use complementary colours – working with a limited palette often gives the most effective results.

KALEIDOSCOPE PATTERNS
 10 MINUTES
 **EASY**

Create a cool Kaleidoscope pattern from your photos with this simple technique.

START HERE

 This technique may be simple but, as you'll discover once you try it, the possibilities are endless, and it's quite addictive trying to find the perfect starting shot.

Also See:
Layers: page 30
Cropping: page 69
Collage and Montage: page 138

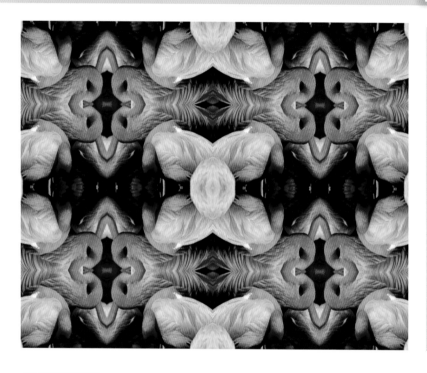

STEP 01

Open your chosen photo in Photoshop and do any basic colour, contrast or brightness tweaks needed. It's a good idea to trim away some of the picture using the **Crop** tool, as you'll get a more abstract result if there's less instantly recognizable detail in the shot.

STEP 02

Turn the Background Layer into a standard editable layer by double-clicking on it in the Layers palette and hitting OK when the **New Layer** dialog appears (the Background Layer is locked by default).

STEP 03

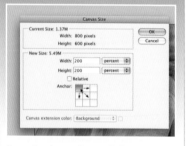

I'm going to produce a 2x2 pattern to start with. Choose **Image>Canvas Size** and increase both horizontal and vertical dimensions to 200%. Use the top left corner for the Anchor point.

STEP 04

Now duplicate the layer containing your photo (**Layer>Duplicate**) three times (so you have a total of four copies).

STEP 05

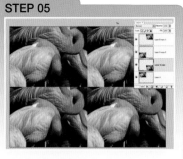

Use the Move tool (keyboard shortcut: V) to position each layer in a corner (they should snap to the edge of the frame, making it easy to position each layer. Use the **Auto-Select** option to select a layer by simply clicking on it.

STEP 06

Use **Edit>Transform>** to flip each layer horizontally (top left copy), vertically (bottom right) and horizontally and vertically (bottom left copy).

STEP 07

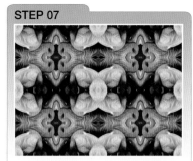

Here, I've merged the four layers into one and repeated the whole process so that the image now contains a total of 16 copies of the original shot.

EXPERIMENTING WITH THE TECHNIQUE

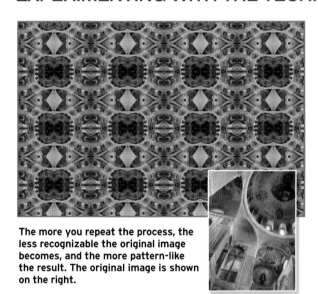

The more you repeat the process, the less recognizable the original image becomes, and the more pattern-like the result. The original image is shown on the right.

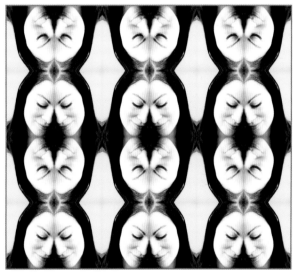

Using faces can be very effective.

Experiment with the positioning of the four quarters for totally different results.

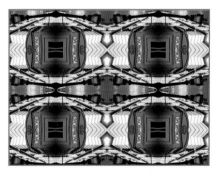

Increase the saturation and contrast for an even bolder effect.

TURN YOUR PHOTOS INTO PAINTINGS AND SKETCHES

Always fancied yourself as a fine artist but lack the skills or time? Then it's time to discover Photoshop's extensive collection of artistic filter effects.

Before you get too excited about the huge list of art effects listed under Photoshop's Filter menu it's worth remembering two things. Firstly, a lot of them, to be frank, aren't very good, and haven't changed for over a decade.

Users who do manage to get convincing natural-media effects out of Photoshop tend to do so by convoluted multi-step processes and a lot of manual intervention, something that could easily fill an entire book. The most successful at doing this are also already skilled artists who use drawing tablets to add their own brushstrokes.

The other issue with Photoshop's filters is that the few that do produce decent single-click results are so over-used that they have gone beyond being merely recognizable to being digital imaging clichés and are therefore best avoided.

That all said, if you do want to turn your photos into paintings or drawings then Photoshop offers a wealth of tools (47 at last count) - and they're a lot easier to experiment with since the introduction of the Filter Gallery in Photoshop CS.

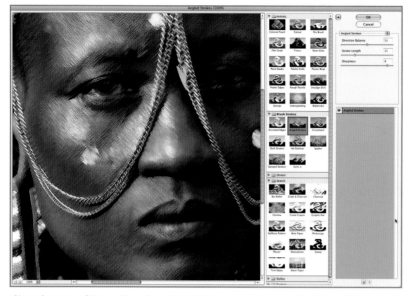

Choosing any of the options from the **Filter** menu brings up the **Filter Gallery**, making it easy to try different effects. **Angled Strokes** is one of the few filters that produces relatively realistic results with a single application.

Some filters, such as **Dark Strokes** (shown here) produce pleasing graphic results – though they don't exactly produce images that look like someone painted them.

With all the filters it's important to experiment with the various sliders as these have a strong effect on the final result.

The **Sketch** effects tend to be more convincing than the paint effects: this is **Chalk and Charcoal**.

All the Sketch effects use the current Foreground and Background Colors, so make sure you set them first or you'll get unexpected results.

Many of the **Artistic/Brush Stroke** effects look more convincing if you add a paper (**Burlap** or **Canvas**) texture after you've applied them (**Filter> Texture>Texturizer**).

ART HISTORY BRUSH DRAWING TECHNIQUE

 30 MINUTES
 ADVANCED

Put Photoshop's Art History Brush to work to produce a realistic chalk drawing.

START HERE

 As it relies more than anything on your own mouse skills, this technique - though simple - is actually quite hard to master. The results, when it works, are certainly worth the effort.

Also See:
Turn Your Photos into Paintings and Sketches: page 126

End Result

Photoshop is not the most well-equipped application when it comes to natural-media filters - paint effects and so on. But there is one tool that can be used to produce some pretty impressive effects with a little practice and the right settings: the Art History Brush.

This kind of treatment works particularly well for strong, simple portraits. This studio shot uses simple, flat lighting and, crucially, a plain undistracting background.

Start Image

Quick Tips

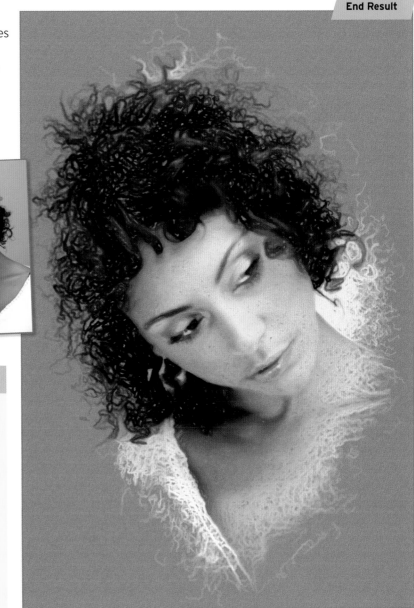

■ Use a smaller brush (down to 1 pixel on small images) and a high Opacity for the most detailed areas.

■ Use the square bracket keys to vary the brush size and the numerical keys (0-9) to vary the Opacity (press 2 for 20% and so on).

■ The Art History Brush works better and is easier to control on lower resolution images.

■ The key to success with the Art History Brush is experimentation and practice.

STEP 01

Start by opening your image in Photoshop. Use **Curves** or **Levels** to boost the contrast. Don't worry about colour – we're not going to see any of it in the final result.

STEP 02

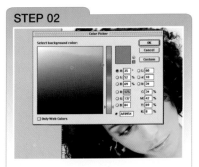

Select a new Background Color by clicking on its swatch at the bottom of the tool bar. When the **Color Picker** appears choose a sepia tone – I'm using R175, G137, B84.

STEP 03

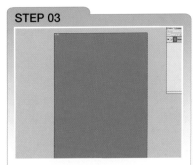

Click OK to accept the new Background Color. Choose **Edit> Select All** and press Ctrl-Delete/⌘ -Delete. This will fill the entire canvas with the Background Color.

STEP 04

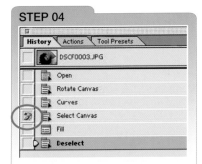

Open the History palette (**Window> History**) and set the source for the **History Brush** by clicking to the left of the Select Canvas step.

STEP 05

Select the **Art History Brush** (hold down the Alt/⌥ key and click on the History Brush. The tool's icon is a brush with a curly line).
You now need to make some changes to the tool options using the bar at the top of the page (shown above):
• Set the **Brush Size** to about 5 pixels;
• **Mode** to **Luminosity** (so you paint only with light and dark, not colour);
• **Opacity** to around 10-15%;
• For the **Style** use **Tight Long**.
• For the **Area** try around 200-400 pixels (it needs to be around one-fifth the width of your image in pixels).
• Leave the **Tolerance** set to 0%.
Note that the Brush Size defines the size of the individual strokes, the Area defines how many strokes are laid down – and over what area – as you paint.

STEP 06

Start by quickly painting around the canvas to roughly establish the outline of your subject. Don't go right to the edges and don't lay down too many strokes – it is easy to overdo this effect at any stage.

STEP 07

Now experiment with different Brush Sizes (smaller for more detailed areas, larger for a smudgy look), Area settings and Opacities to paint in the face. Use the **History** palette to go back if you mess things up too much.

STEP 08

Finally, when you are happy with the result, run the **Texturizer** filter (**Filter >Texture>Texturizer**). Use the **Canvas** texture, with a **Light Direction** Top Left or Top Right. Tweak the **Scaling** and **Relief** settings to your taste.

ADDING BORDERS AND EDGE EFFECTS

Give your images impact with a simple frame or go for something more creative with an edge effect.

It's amazing how the simplest things – such as the addition of a basic border or frame – can have a profound effect on the presentation of your images. There are many, many ways to add borders and frames to your pictures. Feel free to experiment as much as you want, but for my money nothing beats the classic keyline and frame for the perfect finishing touch.

SIMPLE KEYLINES AND BORDERS

The quickest way to add a simple border to an image is to increase the Canvas Size (**Image>Canvas Size**). Set the Background Color on the tool bar to whatever colour you want your border first.

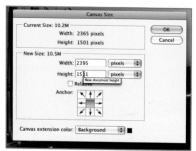

To add a keyline use a Background Color of white and increase the Canvas Size in both directions by the same small number of pixels. Then repeat with black using a larger number of pixels.

Using this method creating multiple keylines is possible – here I've increased the Canvas Size four times in total – white 10 pixels, black 60 pixels, white 10 pixels, then finally black 300 pixels.

For a more flexible approach make the Background Layer editable (by double-clicking on its thumbnail in the Layers palette) and create another layer below it filled with colour.

You can now add a keyline by adding a **Stroke** to the upper layer (using **Layer Styles**, see page 33).

The advantage of working with layers like this is that you can quickly experiment with different keyline and border colours without having to start again from scratch.

DUPLICATE LAYERS AS BORDERS

Try experimenting with duplicate layers to make borders. Here the Background Layer has been blurred and desaturated. A **Stroke** and **Drop Shadow** Layer Style has been applied to a scaled-down duplicate of the original image in a separate layer (use **Edit>Transform>Scale** to shrink the top layer).

LAYER MASK EDGES

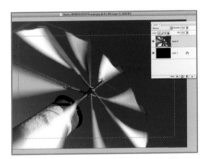

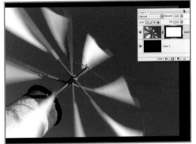

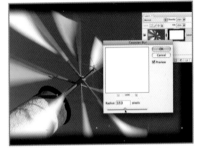

To create edge effects first make the Background Layer editable and place it above a filled layer. Now create a rectangular selection some way in from the edge.

Choose **Layer>Layer Mask>Reveal Selection**. You'll see a border appear where the mask hides the area outside your selection.

You can now edit the Layer Mask in whatever way you choose. Here I'm running a **Gaussian Blur** filter on the mask to give a soft vignette-style edge to my image.

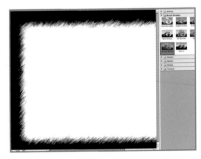

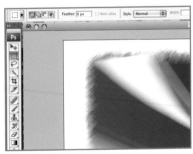

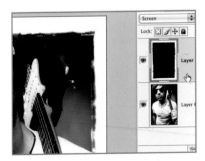

Experiment with the various **Sketch**, **Distort** and **Brush Strokes** filters under the **Filter** menu to give your mask a distressed edge.

The nice thing about using a Layer Mask like this is that you can easily try out different colour fills for the lower layer.

Create a black and white edge image and pop it into a layer above your image. Change the Blending Mode to **Screen** for an instant edge effect. You'll find free masks on the Internet.

TURN DAYTIME INTO NIGHT-TIME

20 MINUTES
ADVANCED

Why venture out at night when Photoshop can easily turn any daytime shot into a moonlit landscape?

START HERE

This technique requires a basic grasp of Layers, Adjustment Layers and Paint tools. It works with almost any kind of scenic shot, but you may need to fine-tune some of the steps.

Also See:
Layer Blending Options: page 34
Adjustment Layers: page 44

STEP 01

We'll start with the overall tone of the picture. Night scenes tend to have virtually no colour information, and a strong blue cast. Choose Layer>New Adjustment Layer>Hue/Saturation. Click on OK when the **New Layer** dialog appears and try the following settings in the **Hue/Saturation** dialog (with the **Colorize** option ticked); Hue 230, Saturation 35, Lightness -40.

End Result

Start Image

STEP 02

Now to add the moon. If you don't have your own shot of the moon you can find one at **www.freedigitalphotos.net/image/s_full-moon.jpg**. Drag it on to your main image using the **Move** tool – it will appear as a new layer.

STEP 03

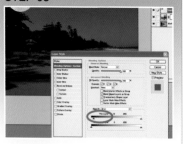

Double-click on the new (moon) layer's thumbnail and when the **Layer Style** window appears you will see the **Blending Options**. Move the shadow slider on the **This Layer** scale a little to the right as shown above. The black part of the layer will disappear.

STEP 04

To make sure the moon looks like it is behind the trees, move the shadow slider for the underlying layer a small amount to the right. Now hold down the Alt (⌥) key to split the slider and drag it a little further along the scale (see above). You should see the branches of the tree showing through.

STEP 05

Now to add some moon lighting. Start by creating a new transparent layer above the Adjustment Layer created in step 01. Using the **Paint Brush** tool choose a large soft brush and 100% white paint and paint on to the new blank layer roughly where you want your moonlight to fall.

STEP 06

Change the Opacity of the new layer to around 60-70% and the Blending Mode to **Overlay**. You should now also move the moonlight layer down below the Hue/Saturation Adjustment Layer. You can now edit the moonlight layer for the most realistic effect using the **Paint Brush** and **Eraser** tools.

STEP 07

Select the Background Layer and **Burn** tool from the tool palette. In the Options bar choose a large soft brush and set the Range to **Shadows**. Use sweeping strokes to darken the top and bottom of the image. I also added some clouds using the same method described in steps 02-03.

ADVANCED ADJUSTMENT LAYER 'NIGHT STREET' EFFECT

With some careful brush work you can create a night street scene full of atmosphere in a couple of steps.

Add a Hue/Saturation Adjustment Layer and use the **Colorize** option with Hue set to 31 and Saturation to 77.

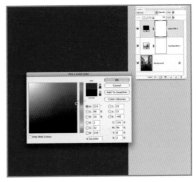

Now add a **Solid Color Fill Layer** and choose a nice dark blue. Set the Blending Mode to **Multiply**.

Set the Foreground Color to black and use a large, soft brush at an Opacity of around 30% on the Color Fill Layer's mask to reveal the orange below where you'd like the light to fall.

To give the streetlight a bit of extra shine, I painted on to the bottom layer using a soft brush and white paint.

FAKE MINIATURE MODEL EFFECT
10 MINUTES
INTERMEDIATE

It's a small world with this simple, but very effective selective blurring effect for producing fake macros.

START HERE

 This technique requires Photoshop CS or later as it uses the Lens Blur filter, and there's not really any other tool capable of producing the same result.

 Also See:
Reducing Depth of Field: page 103
Quick Mask mode: page 27
Cropping: page 69

Start Image

Photographers have long used tilt and shift lenses to change the plane of focus and increase apparent depth of field in close-up shots. But recently it has become fashionable to use them to more creative effect – to turn everyday landscapes into realistic looking fake miniatures or models.

This optical illusion can be remarkably effective and it works by replicating the appearance of a picture taken with very narrow depth of field, something common to extreme close-up photographs. The technique itself is very simple; the key lies in selecting the correct image and cropping it carefully to enhance the illusion.

Choosing (or shooting) the right image is key to this trick of the eye; it needs to be taken from above (as you would shoot a model or miniature) and ideally not be too complex. You also want bright, contrasty sunlight and strong shadows. It's a good idea to crop the image to exclude any sky and to concentrate the viewer's attention on one small part of the scene. Cars are good for this technique, as are people – as long as they're very small in the frame, there aren't too many of them and they aren't too detailed. For this step-by-step example I'm using a shot of the Hoover Dam, which I grabbed very quickly through the window of a helicopter.

End Result

STEP 01

Open the image in Photoshop and crop it roughly if necessary to remove any sky or very distant areas. Enter **Quick Mask** mode by pressing the Q key or clicking on the icon on the tool palette circled above in red.

STEP 02

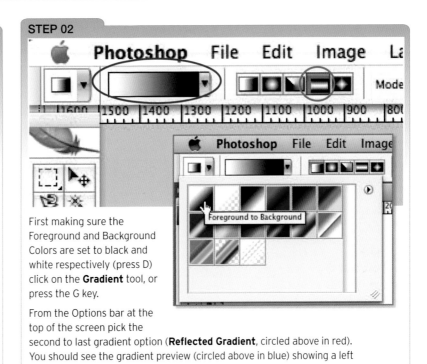

First making sure the Foreground and Background Colors are set to black and white respectively (press D) click on the **Gradient** tool, or press the G key.

From the Options bar at the top of the screen pick the second to last gradient option (**Reflected Gradient**, circled above in red). You should see the gradient preview (circled above in blue) showing a left to right black to white fade. If you don't, click on the little arrow on the right of the Gradient preview and choose the first Preset.

STEP 03

Click with the Gradient tool in the middle of the frame (or wherever you want the point of focus to be) and drag the mouse up towards the top of the frame (it doesn't matter if it's completely straight), then release the mouse button. You should see the gradient appear on the Quick Mask as a red overlay as shown here.

STEP 04

Exit Quick Mask mode (press Q again) and choose **Filter>Blur>Lens Blur**. You'll need to experiment a little with the settings, though the ones I've shown on the screenshot above are a good starting point. When you're happy with the effect press Enter.

Working non-destructively?
You may wonder why I'm not using a separate layer for the blurring, given my constant advice to work in a non-destructive way. The answer is that while you can, the results simply aren't as good. This is because of how the Lens Blur filter does its complex processing.

If you have an active selection (such as we created here) the amount of defocusing will be defined by the selection/mask, with fully selected areas completely out of focus, fully unselected areas completely in focus. Everything in between (the gradient) will be partially blurred, giving the very convincing gradual fall-off in focus.

You can work on a duplicate layer using a mask (the Lens Blur filter allows you to base the **Distance** – how out of focus an area is – on a layer's mask), but you need to then delete this mask to get the effect seen here – you can't edit it as the results end up looking wrong. It is, therefore, slightly futile.

You should also note that if you do want to use a mask as the basis for the blur Distance and create it using the method described on the previous page you will need to click the **Invert** option or you will end up with the wrong section blurred and a completely pointless image.

STEP 05

After a few seconds you should see the result of the Lens Blur filter getting gradually stronger towards the top and bottom of the frame. If you're happy with how it looks get rid of the selection (**Select>Deselect**).

STEP 06

At this point, zoom in and have a look at the result; you may want to crop a little tighter so it looks more like a realistic miniature.

STEP 07

The effect is more convincing if you blow out the highlights slightly. Open the **Curves** dialog (**Image> Adjustments>Curves**) and click on the line roughly a quarter of the way in from the right and drag up slightly, as shown above.

STEP 08

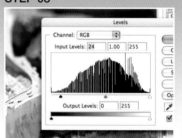

Finally tweak the contrast (here I'm using **Levels**) to ensure the shadows are dark. I also find that some images benefit from a little **Saturation** boost when using this technique.

CHOOSING YOUR SHOT

You can use this technique on almost any shot, but those with a few detailed structures on a fairly plain background seem to work the best.

If you include people in the shot they need to be small enough to be fairly indistinct. Careful cropping is also vital to a realistic effect.

CHAPTER EIGHT

COLLAGE AND MONTAGE

Photoshop's extensive retouching, masking and layering tools make amazing seamless montages possible, but they don't necessarily make them easy. This chapter looks at some of the key tools and techniques needed for convincing montages and pleasing collages – putting them to work, however, is down to you.

Photo-montage covers a huge range of projects, from the very simple (changing backgrounds, putting in new skies, swapping heads) to the incredibly complex; it's not unusual for high-end retouching work to involve dozens of layers and files running into gigabytes. Yet the list of essential skills to get started (all of which have already been covered in depth) is actually fairly short; using layers, making selections, creating and editing Layer Masks and applying tonal adjustments.

However, there are two more must-haves for successful photo-montage and neither can be easily taught (though they can be developed through practice). The first is imagination – without ideas and an eye for composition you'll never produce anything of value. The second, which only really comes from a deep understanding of all the tools in Photoshop's extensive armoury, is the ability to think laterally when faced with problems and to take a completely different approach when needed.

Serious Photoshop artists are constantly on the lookout for new, more efficient or more effective ways to produce the results they're after, and you need to be the same. The Internet is full of people prepared to share their techniques and secrets, so do some research, adapt the ideas you discover and never, ever stop learning.

CREATE A STYLISH TOANED COLLAGE
 30 MINUTES
INTERMEDIATE

Combine a selection of shots in a retro-cinematic style using simple toning techniques.

START HERE

This simple technique requires a basic grasp of layers and the use of the Layers palette. You'll also be using Hue/Saturation controls and creating - and using - Guides.

Also See:
Layers: page 30
Hue/Saturation: page 60
Converting to Black and White: page 94

When combining several shots into a single collage it's easy to end up with a messy clash of colours and shapes. This technique - which works just as well with portraits as it does with cityscapes such as used here - is an altogether classier, cinematic treatment that doesn't take long.

STEP 01

Start by choosing your images; you'll need no more than 6 or 7 shots (and obviously it makes sense if they're all related in some way). Open Photoshop and create a new blank document at the size you intend to print the final collage. I'm using A4 (210 x 297mm / 8.268 x 11.693in) here, but you can use any size.

STEP 02

Open each of your chosen images and crop if necessary, then use the Move tool to drag the photo on to the blank document created in step 01.

STEP 03

You may need to resize the images as you go; click on the new layer and use the **Edit>Free Transform** command to scale them down (hold down the Shift key as you drag the corner handles to retain the original proportions).

STEP 04

Once you've got all the separate elements of the collage into your master document you can start to rearrange them using the Move tool (and the **Free Transform** command to resize as necessary).

STEP 05

It's a good idea to use some guides to get everything to line up neatly. To create guides choose **View>Rulers**. You can now click in either ruler and drag guides on to the image.

STEP 06

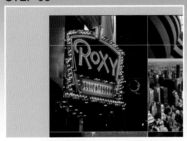

Once you're happy with the layout it's time to start the toning. Make sure the layer you want to work on is selected and choose **Image>Adjustments>Hue/Saturation**. Click on the **Colorize** option and play around with the Hue and Saturation sliders until you get the tone you want (you can always go back and change it later). You'll find a slightly lower Saturation usually produces the most effective results. Repeat the process for each layer. Keep an eye on the harmony of colours.

STEP 07

At this point you can zoom in and tidy up the alignment of each layer using the Move tool. Use **View>Snap** to make aligning to the guides easier and trim away any overlapping areas using the Marquee tool and Delete key. Now to add the white key lines.

STEP 08

Add a new layer (**Layer>New Layer**). Move the new layer to the top of the stack by dragging its thumbnail on the Layers palette. Set the **Foreground Color** to white and select the **Pencil** tool (it makes harder edges than the Paint Brush).

STEP 09

Choose a **Brush Size** of around 10-15 pixels and leave the **Hardness** setting at 100%. You can now paint the dividing lines on to the new blank layer. Hold down the Shift key to keep the lines straight and use the guides to get the position right.

QUICK MULTI-SHOT 'JOINER' COLLAGE

🕐 15 MINUTES
📊 EASY

This is a simple graphic effect for a single image to give the impression it is formed from a series of shots.

START HERE

⚙ This simple but effective treatment is based on David Hockney's 'joiner' photo collage technique (which combines various shots of the same subject into a single patchwork). Take it as a starting point for your own experiments.

🔍 **Also See:**
Layer Styles: page 33
Organizing Layers: page 37

STEP 01

We'll start with this studio portrait, though this effect works well with scenic shots too. Turn the background into an editable layer (double-click on the Background Layer in the Layers palette and click OK when the **New Layer** dialog appears).

STEP 02

Now create a new layer (**Layer>New Layer**) below the layer containing the photo and fill it with white (**Edit>Fill**). Make sure the rulers are visible (**View>Rulers**) and create two guides bisecting the frame horizontally and vertically (to create a guide, click in the ruler and drag on to the image).

STEP 03

Add two more guides to cut the image up into eighths. Make sure the **Snap to Guides** option is turned on (**View>Snap To>All**) and use the Rectangular Marquee tool to select the area in the first segment (the selection will snap to the edges of the frame and the guides).

STEP 04

Choose **Layer>New>Layer via Cut** (or press Shift-Ctrl-J / ⇧-⌘-J). Click on Layer 0 (the main image) again and repeat for each of the segments created using the guides. Always remember to go back to the original layer each time before cutting out a new segment.

STEP 05

One you've finished you can delete the original layer (Layer 0) leaving you with eight layers containing a section of the photo, plus the new white background created in step 02.

STEP 06

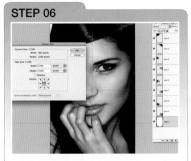

Increase the Canvas Size (**Image> Canvas Size**) by around 30% in both directions. You'll need to re-fill the Background Layer with white to ensure it fills the newly enlarged canvas.

STEP 07

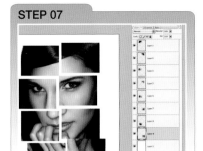

Using the Move tool, select each layer in turn and move each one to get a nicely messy layout. Don't go too far (especially with portraits) – you still want to be able to make out what the photograph is.

STEP 08

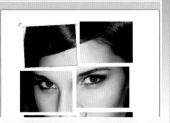

With one of the segment layers selected, choose **Edit>Free Transform** (or press Ctrl-T / ⌘-T). Move your mouse to just outside the layer at one of the corners and the cursor will change to **Rotate** mode. You can now click and drag to rotate the layer.

STEP 09

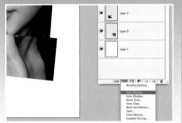

With the top layer selected, choose **Drop Shadow** from the **Layer Effects** drop-down menu at the bottom of the layer palette. If you're using an older version of Photoshop you'll find the Drop Shadow option under the main menu **Layer>Layer Style.**

STEP 10

The exact figures you use here will depend on the size and nature of your image, but an Opacity of around 50% and a **Distance/Size** setting of 5 pixels is good for this 1200x800 shot. Use the preview to judge what settings best suit your own image.

Quick Tips

■ Experiment with more random cutting up of the photo using freehand Selection tools. The basic technique used is the same, but the segments are irregular shapes.

■ Click the Move tool's **Show Transform Controls** option and you can rotate layers without needing to go to a menu each time.

STEP 11

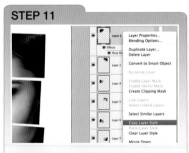

On the Layers palette right-click on the right-hand side of the layer with the drop shadow. From the drop-down menu that appears choose Copy Layer Style. Select all the other segment layers, right-click and choose Paste Layer Style.

STEP 12

An optional final step is to give each of the layers a white border. Using the same technique as for the Drop Shadow, this time adding a **Stroke** (**Size**: 10-20 pixels, **Position**: Inside, **Fill Type**: Color - white).

■ If you're using CS2 or later try using **Edit>Transform>Warp** on each layer. Click and drag any point on the warp mesh to create the impression that the individual prints aren't flat.

PHOTO-MONTAGE TOOLS AND TECHNIQUES

There's no magic formula for creating seamless montages, but there are plenty of techniques to make it easier.

If you've worked your way through the rest of this book before arriving at this point then you should already have picked up most of the basic techniques needed to blend two or more images into a seamless photo-montage. Whether it's something as simple as replacing a boring sky with one that's a little more attractive or a complex composition build from elements taken from multiple source images, the essential process is the same. And – like so many Photoshop techniques – it all comes back to your ability to create accurate selections and Layer Masks. No matter how clever your composition, if you can see the join, the montage won't work (the human eye is notoriously good at spotting anything that doesn't quite match).

As well as seamless masking you need to think about matching the colour, contrast, lighting, perspective and texture of the various elements in a montage. Photoshop offers lots of tools for altering all these, but some (particularly perspective and lighting) require advanced techniques that are best left to the professional digital artist.

But if there's one secret to successful photo-montage – certainly to making your life easier and the process less laboured – it's to get the pictures right at the capture stage. Planning an image before you start shooting will almost guarantee you save time later – especially if you shoot plenty of minor variations of framing and lighting. It's a lot easier to mask something that

Unfortunately not every selection or mask is as easy to create as the one shown on the opposite page.

A trick is to find the channel with the greatest contrast between subject and background and to duplicate it to form the basis of a mask.

Edit this new channel using **Levels** to increase the contrast and **Brush** tools (including Dodge and Burn tools) to create a perfect mask. It takes a lot of time and practice.

When finished use Select>Load Selection to load the new channel into a selection (which can then in turn be turned into a Layer Mask).

This technique (and variations on it) can be used to create masks for highly complex subjects, as long as the background isn't too cluttered.

Tools such as Liquify (Filter>Liquify) (above) and the various options under the Edit>Transform menu (right) allow you to easily and quickly distort, rotate, resize, flip or warp layers for perfect seamless blends or special effects.

has been photographed against a plain background, and it's a lot easier to combine several images if they were all shot from the same position with the same lighting. This is why so many complex commercial montages start out not in Photoshop, but in a photographic studio with a sketch and highly controlled lighting.

But of course the ideal world and the real world are very different places, and few amateur Photoshoppers have the resources or the time to plan every montage in advance. Nor would they want to; half the fun of photo-montage is finding ways of combining the photographs you've already got in ways that you never imagined when you took them. And this is where your eye for composition, your selection and masking skills and your knowledge of the various cheats and shortcuts Photoshop offers will grow the more you practice your montage technique.

Key Tools

Although a complex montage could involve virtually every tool and technique in this book, the key tools essential to all montage work are Layers (so you can manipulate the various elements independently), Selections and Masks (so you can hide the parts of each layer you don't want to see) and the Transformation tools (mostly found under the **Edit>Transform** menu), needed to scale, distort, rotate and – with later versions of Photoshop – warp the individual layers. Since you're probably going to need to match the various elements tonally, it's

SIMPLE MONTAGES WITH MASKS

There's no need for complex selections when working with plain white backgrounds; the perfect Layer Mask is only a few brushstrokes away.

To montage these two images together, first I need to drag them both into the same Photoshop document as separate layers.

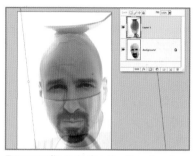

Temporarily reducing the Opacity of the top layer makes it easier to see what I'm doing as I rotate it (using **Edit>Transform>Free Transform**).

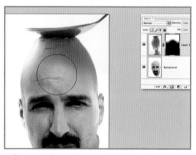

After adding a Layer Mask to the upper layer, all I need is a large soft brush to paint black on to the mask in the areas I want to hide.

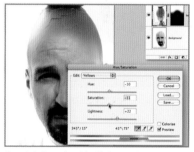

A quick tweak of both layers' brightness, contrast and colour, evens out any slight tonal mismatch.

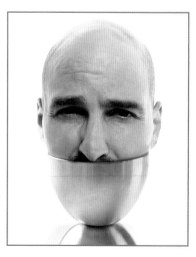

The end result after a few minutes' work; two montages using a couple of images and a very simple hand-drawn Layer Mask.

Tool Tip: Extract

Photoshop's **Extract** Tool (Filter>
Extract) makes the process of
cutting out complex or ill-defined
subjects (such as fur) easier. It's not
foolproof but is worth a try when
faced with a seemingly impossible
selection job.

1: Defining the area to be extracted

Use the **Highlighter** tool to paint
the edge of the area to be extracted.
The smaller the brush and the closer
you trace the edge the better. For
indistinct areas use a larger brush,
and for well-defined edges use the
Smart Highlighting option.

With the edge drawn, use the **Fill** tool
to define the area to retain.

2: Refining the extraction

Click on **Preview** and choose a **Display
Mode**. Use the **Cleanup** tool to
make areas of the mask opaque or
transparent and the **Touchup** tool
to clean up the edges, then click OK.

Photoshop will delete
(not mask) areas outside
the extraction, so work
on a duplicate. You'll
probably need to refine the
extraction before you can
add your new background.

rare for even a simple background
swap not to require the use of
at least one of the adjustments
covered in pages 48–63.

If you're working on anything
particularly involved you'll also
want to make use of Photoshop's
Layer Comps (see opposite) and,
perhaps more importantly, the
History and Snapshot features
(page 18), which allow you to step
back to an earlier stage in the
process when things go wrong.

Ultimately, if you want to get
really good at photo-montage

you're going to have to master
pretty much everything in
Photoshop's extensive toolbox.
Once you've perfected your
masking and layering skills you'll
need to understand how the
various tools and techniques can
solve the inevitable unexpected
problems you come across in the
process. On these pages, and in the
step-by-step projects that follow,
I've tried to cover the basics you'll
need to get started, but in such a
small space this can only ever hope
to scratch the surface.

SELECTING LAYERS

**When you've got more than a few layers in a montage it makes sense to
learn some tricks for more easily selecting the one(s) you want to work on.**

Right-click on the image itself with the
Move tool for a pop-up list of every
layer under the mouse pointer. If you
hold down the Ctrl (⌘) key while using
any other tool you can temporarily
switch to the Move tool (so if you Ctrl/
⌘-right-click using the Brush you'll see
this menu appear).

Choose **Auto-Select** from the Move
tool's options and you can simply click
on a layer on the image itself to select
it. Since CS2 you can also Shift-click to
select more than one Layer.

If you don't have the Auto-Select
option on (it can get in the way
sometimes), hold the Alt (⍉) key while
right-clicking on a layer to select it (if
you're not using the Move tool Ctrl-Alt
/ ⌘-⍉ will select any layer you right-
click on).

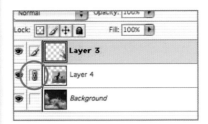

In Photoshop CS and earlier if you want
to move or transform more than one
layer simultaneously you need to link
them first.

More modern versions allow you to
Ctrl/⌘-click on the layer names in the
Layers palette to select multiple layers.
Shift-click to select a range.

EDITING MASKS

You'll find plenty of Layer Mask tips throughout this book. Here are a few that are particularly useful in photo-montage projects.

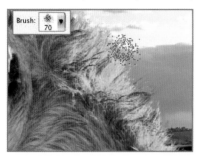

Some very fine textures, such as fur, can be all but impossible to mask using conventional Selection tools.

Instead, use one of Photoshop's built-in **Spatter Brush** Presets (or create your own) on the Layer Mask.

You can use the standard image adjustments on a Layer Mask – here I've made a selection on the mask itself and am reducing the contrast to create a semi-transparent area.

If you want to check the accuracy of your mask, add a temporary duplicate layer directly underneath (without a mask) and invert it. Any stray pixels will now show up in sharp relief.

USING LAYER COMPS (CS+)

An easy way to experiment with layouts without producing huge files.

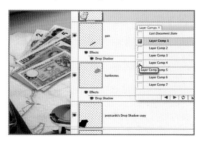

We looked at the **History** feature on page 99, but there is an alternative that's useful when experimenting with multi-layered compositions. **Layer Comps** (Window>Layer Comps) are like snapshots of the Layers palette, remembering the visibility, appearance (Layer Styles) and position of all your layers, so you can go back and compare your layouts as you try different things. Unlike History, Layer Comps are saved as .PSD files and don't take up much disk space.

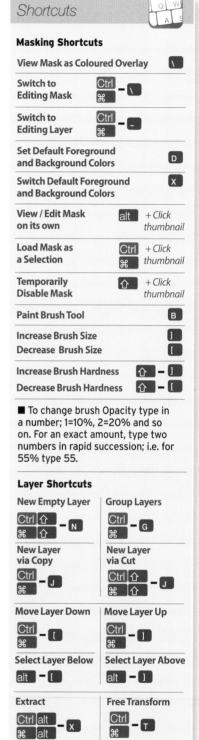

Shortcuts

Masking Shortcuts

View Mask as Coloured Overlay	\
Switch to Editing Mask	Ctrl/⌘ – \
Switch to Editing Layer	Ctrl/⌘ – ~
Set Default Foreground and Background Colors	D
Switch Default Foreground and Background Colors	X
View / Edit Mask on its own	alt + Click thumbnail
Load Mask as a Selection	Ctrl/⌘ + Click thumbnail
Temporarily Disable Mask	⇧ + Click thumbnail
Paint Brush Tool	B
Increase Brush Size	]
Decrease Brush Size	[
Increase Brush Hardness	⇧ –]
Decrease Brush Hardness	⇧ – [

■ To change brush Opacity type in a number; 1=10%, 2=20% and so on. For an exact amount, type two numbers in rapid succession; i.e. for 55% type 55.

Layer Shortcuts

New Empty Layer	Group Layers
Ctrl ⇧ / ⌘ ⇧ – N	Ctrl / ⌘ – G
New Layer via Copy	**New Layer via Cut**
Ctrl / ⌘ – J	Ctrl ⇧ / ⌘ ⇧ – J
Move Layer Down	**Move Layer Up**
Ctrl / ⌘ – [	Ctrl / ⌘ –]
Select Layer Below	**Select Layer Above**
alt – [	alt –]
Extract	**Free Transform**
Ctrl alt / ⌘ alt – X	Ctrl / ⌘ – T

■ With the Move tool active you can nudge layers using the arrow keys. Hold down the Alt (⌥) key as you nudge to create a duplicate layer.

PHOTO-MONTAGE STEP-BY-STEP
45 MINUTES
ADVANCED

Time to put everything we've learned to use in this long-winded but straightforward photo-montage.

START HERE

This is a fairly involved montage project that presumes you're using the exact same images I am (although the techniques can easily be adapted). To find out how to download all the images used see page 5.

Also See:
Montage Techniques: page 142
Layers and Masks: pages 29-46

End Result

Start Images

When shooting for montage it is best to use flat lighting wherever possible (it's easier to add shadows than remove them). The same goes for focus – more depth of field is better, as it's a lot easier to soften than to sharpen. The exception here is the facial close-up, which is out of focus as it will be in the final composition.

This project – and it's a long one – is designed to walk you through the various Photoshop techniques used to cut out and combine several elements into a single image. We're not looking for photo-reality here, simply a result where the first thing you see is the image, not the montage work. To make sure this happens we need to ensure the various elements work together seamlessly. As for the artistic merit of the end result – I'll leave that up to you to decide.

STEP 01

We'll begin with the wall image. First, we need to change the Background Layer to a normal, editable layer. Double-click on it in the Layers palette and when the **New Layer** dialog appears click OK.

STEP 02

Now to make the hole in the wall. Use the **Lasso** tool to create a freehand selection (it will look more natural if it's hand-drawn), following the pattern of bricks. Don't worry about getting it perfect, we'll be changing it later on.

STEP 03

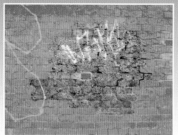

Press Q to **Edit in Quick Mask Mode** and use a hard-edged Paint Brush to tidy up the selection where needed. Remember, black paint removes areas from the selection, white paint adds to the selection (see page 27).

STEP 04

Once you are happy press Q again to return to normal Selection mode. To make the hole you could just press the Delete key, but it's a bit early in the process to be making such permanent changes, so choose **Layer>Add Layer Mask>Hide Selection**. You should see the checkerboard indicating the transparent areas that have been masked. Save the wall image as a new Photoshop document.

STEP 05

Now open the face photo without closing the wall image. I tweaked the colour and contrast slightly, and increased Saturation (**Image> Adjustments>Hue/Saturation**).

STEP 06

Click on the layer thumbnail for the face image and drag and drop it on to the wall image. This will create a new layer containing the face in the Photoshop file.

STEP 07

By default the new layer will be at the top of the stack – above the wall layer. Click on the face layer's thumbnail in the Layers palette and drag it to below the wall.

STEP 08

Now to add the hands. Open the first shot and use the **Magic Wand** to select the black area. Hold down the Shift key and keep clicking in the areas around the hand until you have roughly selected the entire background.

STEP 09

Choose **Select>Modify>Smooth...** and enter a setting of 2 pixels. Now choose **Select>Modify>Expand...** and again enter a setting of 2 pixels. This will help to remove the halo you often get when using the Magic Wand.

STEP 10

Once you are happy you have a relatively accurate selection, promote the Background Layer to an editable layer and add a **Layer Mask** hiding the selection (because we selected the background, not the hand itself).

STEP 11

As in step 06, drag the hand layer from the Layers palette on to your montage. It will inevitably need some resizing to make it fit. Use **Edit>Transform>Scale** and click and drag one of the corner handles to resize the layer.

STEP 12

Repeat the process (steps 08-11) for the other hand. Add a **Drop Shadow** to both hand layers (**Layer>Layer Style>Drop Shadow**). Use the preview to pick the right settings (you can always change them later).

STEP 13

Finally, tweak the colour/contrast of each hand layer to match the rest of the scene. In this case I simply darkened the mid-tones by moving the middle slider in **Levels** (**Image> Adjustments>Levels**) to the right.

STEP 14

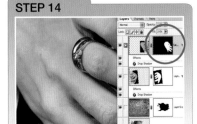

Now to start cleaning up the edges of those hands, which on close inspection are hardly seamless. We'll do this by editing each layer's mask. To start editing the mask, first we need to click on its thumbnail in the Layers palette.

STEP 15

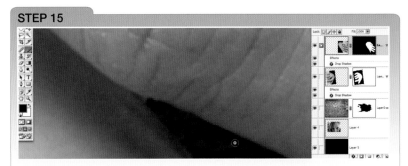

Select the Paint Brush tool and choose a small (5- or 6-pixel) Brush Size from the Options bar at the top of the screen. It's also probably better not to use a really hard-edged brush. Zoom right in to the image (200% or more) and start to paint the mask for a better edge. Remember, black paint hides more of the layer, white paint reveals more. Use a softer, large brush for the edge on the back of the hand where it overlaps the out-of-focus face, this will help to blend it more seamlessly.

STEP 16

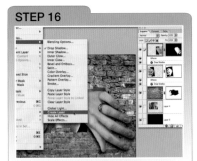

When you've cleaned up the edges of both hands (this could take a while), select each hand layer in turn and choose **Layer>Layer Style>Create Layer**. If a warning appears just click on OK – it isn't relevant in this case.

STEP 17

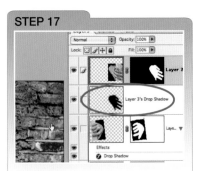

If you look at the Layers palette you will see that the Drop Shadow is now in a layer of its own. This allows you to carefully erase any areas where it doesn't look natural.

STEP 18

Now to add some depth to the wall so it looks less like a cardboard cut-out. Click on the wall layer in the Layers palette and choose **Layer>Duplicate** (or press Ctrl-J / ⌘-J).

STEP 19

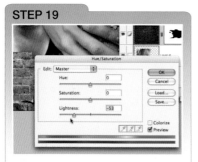

Make sure the lower of the two wall layers is selected and choose **Image> Adjustments>Hue/Saturation**. Reduce the **Lightness** - a setting of about -50 should darken it enough for our purposes.

STEP 20

We now need to unlink the darkened wall layer's mask from the layer itself - so we can move it independently. Click on the little link icon between the two thumbnails as shown above. Now click on the mask thumbnail, select the **Move** tool (press V) and use the left arrow key to nudge the mask about 10 or 20 pixels to the left. You may need to edit the mask of the darkened layer (as shown here) to make the ends of the bricks look more realistic.

STEP 21

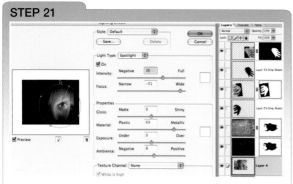

To give the impression that it is darker behind the wall than outside I'm going to use **Lighting Effects** (**Filter>Render> Lighting Effects**) to add a spotlight effect. Select the face layer in the Layers palette and use the settings shown above.

STEP 22

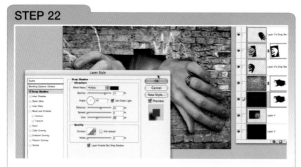

Finally, we need to add a shadow from the wall on to the face. Select the lower (darkened) copy of the wall layer and choose **Layer>Layer Style>Drop Shadow...** Use a size of around 90 pixels and a distance of 65 pixels. All you need do now is to zoom in and examine your work carefully, tidying up wherever necessary.

Quick Tips

■ Although this project contains all the steps necessary to produce the montage shown on the first page it is up to you to fine-tune the final image to get it exactly right. In fact, if you're prepared to spend a little time on it you should be able to improve on my effort.

■ Check that the colour and contrast of all four elements match as closely as possible.

■ Texture is just as important; though the four elements were all shot digitally, I used three different cameras, each having its own unique feel. To disguise the differences try adding a non-destructive texture layer. Here's how:

(i) Go to Layer>New>Layer.
(ii) In the **New Layer** dialog set the Blending Mode to **Overlay** and tick the **Fill with Overlay Neutral Color** option
(iii) Make sure that the new layer is at the top of the stack in the Layers palette and add some noise using the Filter>Noise>Add Noise command.

■ To add a sense of scale to the final image, try adding another element - a bicycle or perhaps a post box - to make the emerging hands seem giant.

■ Always save a layered (.PSD) copy of your montage - even if you flatten the file in order to save it in JPEG or TIFF format. That way you can always go back and make changes in the future without starting from scratch.

■ Save any overall changes - such as adding texture, sharpening or altering global colour/contrast tweaks until last - and always work on a copy of your finished montage (especially if you flatten it).

'OUT OF FRAME' MONTAGE TECHNIQUE

⏱ **30 MINUTES**
▦ **ADVANCED**

Give any image a three-dimensional makeover with this popular 'out of bounds' treatment.

START HERE

⚙ Although it may initially seem like a very simple technique, if you want to include realistic shadows there's more to it than meets the eye. You'll also need to be fully confident in the creation and manipulation of masks.

🔍 **Also See:**
Layer Masks: page 39
Montage Techniques: page 142

Start Image

End Result

Although this effect can be used on just about any shot, it works a lot better with a photo such as this, with something obvious to 'jump out' of the frame. The success of the illusion depends on your selecting and masking skills more than anything else.

STEP 01

Duplicate the Background Layer, then turn the background into an editable layer by double-clicking on its thumbnail in the Layers palette (when the **New Layer** dialog appears just click OK).

STEP 02

Draw a rectangular selection (shown here in red) using the **Rectangular Marquee**. This will set the boundary of the frame so will define the parts of the image that end up 'out of bounds'.

STEP 03

Choose **Select>Transform Selection** and hold down the Ctrl (⌘) key as you click and drag each of the corners to distort the rectangle. You're looking for a perspective effect so need to match it to the scene (as shown).

STEP 04

Temporarily hide the upper layer and select the lower layer (click on it in the Layers palette). With the selection created in steps 02 and 03 still active, click on the **Add Layer Mask** icon at the bottom of the Layers palette.

STEP 05

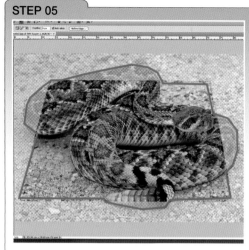

Make the upper layer visible again and reduce its Opacity to 50% (to make it easier to see what you're doing). Using the semi-transparent frame as a guide, use the **Polygonal Lasso** tool to create a rough selection around the areas of the subject which are going to come out of the frame, keeping inside the frame for the rest of the selection (as shown here in red).

STEP 06

Return the Opacity of the upper layer to 100%. Add a Layer Mask to the upper layer based on the selection you just made.

STEP 07

Click on the upper layer's thumbnail (circled above in red) and select the **Paint Brush** tool (keyboard shortcut: B). Select a small Brush Size and set the Hardness to 100%.

STEP 08

Using black paint on the mask, carefully refine the outline of all the areas that fall outside the frame.

STEP 09

As always when working on a mask, if you accidentally hide too much of the layer you can switch to a Foreground Color of white and paint to reveal. Work your way around the entire image to produce a perfect edge.

STEP 10

When you're happy you've got it right create a new layer (Ctrl-Shift-N / ⌘-⇧-N) and fill it with white (the quickest way to do this is to press D to set the Background Color, then Ctrl-Delete / ⌘-⌫ to fill).

STEP 11

Create another new layer and put it below the two snake layers (and above the new white background). Use a large, soft **Paint Brush** to create shadows under the areas where the snake comes out of the frame.

STEP 12

This is the shadow layer I created in step 11 (I've temporarily hidden the upper two layers so you can only see the bottom two. As you can see it's very simple – just a few brushstrokes. Obviously your shadows – if any – will be different depending on the image you're using. Reduce the Opacity of this layer to around 20%.

STEP 13

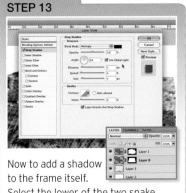

Now to add a shadow to the frame itself.
Select the lower of the two snake layers and add a **Drop Shadow** (**Layer>Layer Style>Drop Shadow**). As this is supposed to look like a sheet of paper on the ground, I'm creating a very small shadow with a small Distance setting (**Distance**: 5 pixels, **Spread**: 0%, **Size**: 7 pixels).

STEP 14

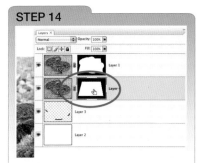

As an optional finishing touch on this project I decided I wanted the frame to have a white border. If you want to give it a try get rid of (or hide) the drop shadow created in step 13. Hold the Ctrl (⌘) key and click on the lower snake layer's mask, this will create a selection based on the mask.

STEP 15

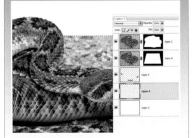

With the selection created in step 14 still active, click on the bottom layer and choose **Layer>New Layer**. This will create a blank transparent layer above the background. Choose **Edit>Fill** and fill the selection with white colour. Choose **Select>Deselect**. Add a **Drop Shadow** to this new layer (as per step 13).

Finally Choose **Edit>Transform>Free Transform** and drag each corner of the layer out to make it large enough to create a border.

EXPERIMENTING WITH THIS TECHNIQUE

This is one of those techniques that once mastered can be adapted and developed in new ways to work with almost any image.

Some subjects will require a vertical frame, but the technique is identical.

In all these examples, the plain white background has been replaced.

Here, a more ornate frame has been used, along with a carefully painted shadow that adds to the three-dimensional quality and realism of the effect.

CHAPTER NINE

BRIDGE AND CAMERA RAW

They may have arrived fairly late on the scene, but both Adobe Bridge and Camera Raw have grown and developed at a remarkable pace, with the former now spun off into a fully-fledged application in its own right and the latter gaining new and more refined tools with every update.

Adobe Bridge started life as the File Browser, a feature introduced in Photoshop 7.0 and refined in Photoshop CS. The File Browser was – and remains for those using older versions – a rather slow, somewhat limited, but nonetheless quite useful digital light box for browsing thumbnails. It has rudimentary sorting, ranking and renaming features and on a modern computer it feels a lot faster (in 2002 when Photoshop 7.0 was launched the hardware wasn't up to it). Because the File Browser was running inside Photoshop it also had a negative impact on the performance of the program, which is far from ideal.

And so, with the launch of Photoshop CS2 came Bridge, a stand-alone application that

– although ostensibly designed to tie together the various parts of the Creative Suite - is also developing into a powerful workflow tool in its own right, and one that is particularly useful to the digital photographer.

The Camera Raw Plug-In was first bundled with Photoshop CS. Since then it has grown into one of the most comprehensively featured (and popular) Raw file converters in the world. It has been closely integrated into Bridge, even allowing JPEG files to benefit from its simple but powerful toolset and clean user interface. But it is when working with digital camera Raw files that Camera Raw really shines and if you own a digital SLR and have never shot Raw then you don't know what you're missing.

153

ADOBE CAMERA RAW AND BRIDGE BASICS

Even if you don't shoot raw or have huge collections of images take a moment to get to know these useful Photoshop add-ons; you won't regret it.

Bridge and Camera Raw could each fill several chapters of this book, and on these few pages I can only give a brief description of what they are and what they do. As mentioned in the chapter introduction, they have both seen significant development in the last few years, and in the case of Bridge in particular, each new version has brought important new features and performance improvements. If you're using Photoshop 7.0 or CS then you're stuck with the File Browser, and to be frank there are better browsing and file renaming applications out there that won't impact on the performance of Photoshop.

Bridge didn't really come of age until Photoshop CS3, when new features such as side-by-side multi-image previews, Stacks, the Magnifying Loupe, impressive filtering capabilities, and the upgraded slide show and image import functions, made it a viable alternative to dedicated workflow programs. See the opposite page for a rundown of some of Bridge CS3 and CS4's more useful functions.

So what do you use Bridge for? Primarily, it's still a file browser at heart, albeit one with an ever-growing set of additional features. It's a great way to sort through images before you start working

Adobe Camera Raw 2.x was the first to be bundled free with Photoshop (CS).

on them in Photoshop, and the rating and labelling system makes choosing between lots of similar images a great deal easier. It's also very useful for applying Camera Raw development settings to Raw files without having to open or save them in Photoshop.

BRIDGE EVOLUTION

From slow, underpowered thumbnail browser to fast, sleek and powerful workflow tool for the digital photographer, Bridge has grown up fast.

The **File Browser** in Photoshop 7.0 was pretty useless. It got better in CS (above) but the functionality is very basic - though you can search, sort, batch process and rate images.

The first version of **Bridge** (bundled with CS2) is much more sophisticated, with flexible layouts, Camera Raw integration, scalable thumbnails and a lot besides. What's more, it's no longer a floating window in Photoshop.

CS3 brought a raft of useful new features, a new look and a huge performance boost. Before CS3, I - like many photographers - had ignored Bridge, but it's now my file browser of choice.

154

BRIDGE CS3/CS4 FEATURES

The first truly essential version of Bridge came bundled with Photoshop CS3, and it just keeps getting better.

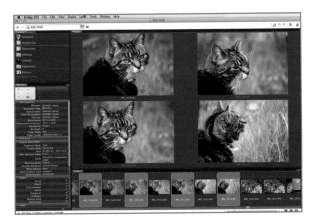

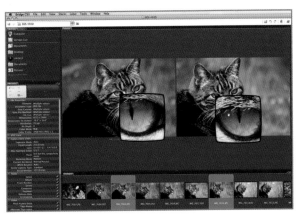

Bridge now has a range of pre-baked layouts (this is the **Filmstrip** view). By selecting multiple thumbnails you can view several preview images side-by-side.

The new **Magnifying Loupe** shows 100–800% view (just click on the preview and scroll to zoom). Hold down the Ctrl (⌘) key to link multiple Loupes and move them together – great for comparing images.

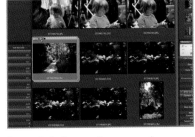

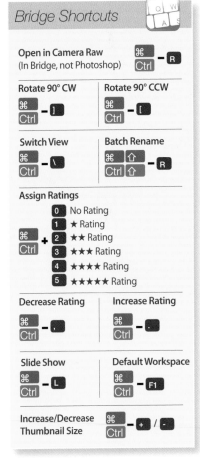

Any image - Raw or JPEG - can be opened in **Camera Raw** inside Bridge (without troubling Photoshop). In Bridge CS4, Raw development settings can be copied between files.

Several photos can be grouped together into a **Stack** (sharing a single thumbnail) - this is useful when browsing large numbers of images in a single folder.

Bridge Shortcuts

Open in Camera Raw
(In Bridge, not Photoshop)
⌘ / Ctrl – R

Rotate 90° CW	**Rotate 90° CCW**
⌘ / Ctrl –]	⌘ / Ctrl – [

Switch View	**Batch Rename**
⌘ / Ctrl – \	⌘ / Ctrl ⇧ – R

Assign Ratings

⌘ / Ctrl +
0	No Rating
1	★ Rating
2	★★ Rating
3	★★★ Rating
4	★★★★ Rating
5	★★★★★ Rating

Decrease Rating	**Increase Rating**
⌘ / Ctrl – ,	⌘ / Ctrl – .

Slide Show	**Default Workspace**
⌘ / Ctrl – L	⌘ / Ctrl – F1

Increase/Decrease Thumbnail Size	⌘ / Ctrl – + / -

Bridge has always had batch renaming capabilities, and in the latest version there are plenty of new options, though dedicated applications that do this are still more powerful.

The **Slide Show** is a fast way to browse images full-screen. Click with the mouse to jump to 100% and press numbers 1-5 to assign ratings.

Adobe Camera Raw (ACR) is a Plug-In that allows Photoshop to open and process the raw (unprocessed) files from digital cameras (without ACR). Shooting Raw (as opposed to JPEG) brings many benefits to the more serious photographer. These include the ability to change parameters such as white balance and sharpening after the shot has been taken. Because you get to play with all the data captured by the sensor (as opposed to the data after the camera has done its processing and JPEG conversion) Raw files are considerably more pliable than JPEGs, and they can effectively be manipulated in a non-destructive way. You also get to import digital camera shots as 16-bit files, something of great importance to professional photographers using high-end equipment.

Most (though not all) of ACR's tonal controls are also available in Photoshop, but the simple, focused interface means many photographers use ACR to do the majority of their basic corrections, only moving to Photoshop when they need the more advanced tools. This is no doubt the reason for the popularity of Adobe's Lightroom (which builds on the functionality of Bridge and ACR).

ADOBE CAMERA RAW ESSENTIALS

As long as the camera model is supported, opening any Raw file in Photoshop (or Bridge) will fire up the **Camera Raw Window**. You'll see between three and eight panels of controls. Some are specific to ACR (such as **White Balance**), others mimic Photoshop adjustments.

ACR has simple **Unsharp Masking** and **Noise Reduction** sliders (I personally let ACR do my noise reduction but use Photoshop for sharpening).

When you've finished you have the choice of opening the image in Photoshop or converting directly into a new file in a format of your choice. If you're using ACR in Bridge, clicking **Done** saves the development settings back into the Raw file (but doesn't convert or open the file).

Later versions of ACR allow you to open several Raw files at once and apply the same settings to them all or work on them individually. You can also save development Presets for use on future photos.

Newer versions of ACR have non-destructive healing tools for removing dust spots and red-eye and a very handy straightening tool. There's also a black and white conversion option.

Camera Raw 5.0 (Photoshop CS4) takes things even further with its new **Adjustment Brush** and **Gradient** tools offering non-destructive localized correction of Raw files.

APPENDIX 1: AUTOMATING PHOTOSHOP WITH ACTIONS

There are many repetitive tasks in image editing. A lot of digital camera users open every file and run a certain set of processes – Auto Levels, sharpen, change resolution and so on – before saving each picture as a TIFF with a more descriptive name than the serial number that the camera assigns.

If you shoot a lot of pictures, this process can become laborious to say the least, and this is where Photoshop's Actions come in. Actions are recordable processes (similar to Macros in word processors and spreadsheets) that can be played back on single files or groups of pictures using a Batch Process. You can record most – though not all – Photoshop commands in an Action and they can be as simple or complex as you want. Actions can even be saved as Droplets (stand-alone applications that will open Photoshop and run an Action on one or more files dropped on to them).

What to use them for

Actions are so powerful that they can be used for an almost limitless variety of jobs, from the aforementioned batch processing of digital camera files, to adding watermarks, to creating web thumbnails. Other uses for Actions include adding keyboard shortcuts to commands that don't already have them (such as changing colour mode or selecting a specific filter or effect). Actions can be fully automatic (you don't enter any values for any of the steps) or can require user intervention to enter values in dialog boxes where necessary. You can also create an Action to automate complex multi-layered artistic effects that you particularly like – online retouching communities are full of people sharing Actions that create special effects.

What can you automate?

You can record most – but not all – Photoshop commands in an Action. You can include virtually all menu commands, selections (Marquee, Magic Wand etc.), type, the Paint Bucket, Gradient and Magic Eraser and all the commands you perform in the Paths, Channels, Layers, Styles, Color, Swatches, History and Actions palettes. What you cannot record are brushstrokes (painting, Rubber Stamping etc.), the creation of Paths (except automatically from a selection), View options, Window tools and Tools options (but some of these can be added to an Action after it has been recorded using the Inset Menu Item option).

The **File>Automate>Batch** menu allows you to run any Action on a folder of images and includes options for the Source and Destination folders, plus automatic renaming of files. You can create a stand-alone Droplet from any Action using the command **File>Automate>Create Droplet.**

Creating an Action

Generating an Action consists of two steps – creating the Action and recording it (for which you'll need to have a picture open in Photoshop). Start by opening an image and making the Actions palette visible (**View>Actions**). Then make a new empty Action set (click on the icon shown above).

Give the new set a name – I've called it Simon's actions. With the new set selected in the Actions palette click on the **New Action** icon. You'll see the New Action dialog appear. Give the Action a name and assign a shortcut if you wish. Click **Record**.

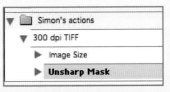

Each step you perform appears in the list under the Action you are recording. Here I've run the **Unsharp Mask** filter after changing the image resolution.

Save and **Save As** steps also appear in the Action if you want them. Once you've finished click on the **Stop** button at the bottom of the Actions palette. You can now play this Action on any open file with the **Play** button.

APPENDIX 2: TIPS AND TRICKS

Part of the fun of using Photoshop is the fact that no matter how long you've been using it there's always something new to learn. This is partly because Photoshop has got so big and so complex, and partly because so many of the really cool little tricks and time savers are not that well documented – if at all. I could fill page after page with keyboard shortcuts power users love, but I've run out of space, so to get you started here are a few tips and tricks that I think are the most useful.

 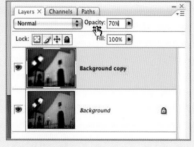 

There's little in Photoshop that can't be controlled by a keyboard shortcut, and you can check them all out via **Edit>Keyboard Shortcuts** (Ctrl-Shift-Alt-K / ⌘-⇧-⌥-K). Click **Summarize** for a nice web page showing all of them.

Photoshop offers several ways to change any numerical value:

■ Click in the Input box, hold down the Ctrl (⌘) key and drag left or right to increase/decrease.
■ Click in the Input box and use the arrow keys to increase/decrease.
■ Click in the Input box and your mouse scroll to increase/decrease.
In all cases, hold down the Shift key at the same time to change the value in increments of 10.

SELECTION TIPS

Marquee tool modifiers (with no current selection):
■ **Alt** (⌥): Create selection centred on first point clicked.
■ **Shift**: Constrain proportions (creates perfect circles or squares).

Selection shortcuts:
■ **Shift**: Add to selection.
■ **Alt** (⌥): Remove from selection.
■ **Ctrl-H** (⌘-H): Hide selection outline (marching ants).
■ **Ctrl-Shift-I** (⌘-⇧-I): Invert selection.
■ **Ctrl-Alt-D** (⌘-⌥-D): Feather selection.

■ If you're using the Marquee tools you can move the selection as you're making it by holding down the Space Bar (without letting go of of the mouse button).

■ When using the Freehand Lasso or Magnetic Lasso hold down the Alt (⌥) key and click to temporarily change to the Polygonal Lasso.

LAYERS TIPS

Blending Mode shortcuts:
■ **Alt-Shift-(plus) and Alt-Shift-(minus)** (⌥-⇧-+ and ⌥-⇧--):
Cycle through Blending Modes for current layer.

■ **Alt-Shift** (⌥-⇧) and the following letters give direct access to Blending Modes: **C**: Color, **N**: Normal, **M**: Multiply, **S**: Screen, **W**: Linear Dodge, **E**: Difference, **T**: Saturation, **Y**: Luminosity, **U**: Hue, **I**: Dissolve, **O**: Overlay, **A**: Linear Burn, **D**: Color Dodge, **F**: Soft Light, **G**: Lighten, **H**: Hard Light, **J**: Linear Light, **K**: Darken, **L**: Hard Mix, **Z**: Pin Light, **X**: Exclusion, **V**: Vivid Light, **B**: Color Burn.

Fill shortcuts:
■ **Alt-Backspace / ⌥-⌫**
Fill with Foreground Color.
■ **Ctrl-Backspace / ⌘-⌫**
Fill with Background Color.
■ **Ctrl-Alt-Backspace / ⌘-⌥-⌫**
Fill with current History state.

In all cases, add the Shift key to preserve transparency when filling.

INDEX

ONLINE RESOURCES

As well as the many books and magazine articles on Photoshop, there are many free resources on the world wide web.

www.photoshopforums.com
Large active community of Photoshop users.

www.photoshopnews.com
News and links.

www.atncentral.com
Large collection of user-generated Actions.

www.pslover.com
Huge collection of user-generated tutorials.

www.getthemostfromphotoshop.com
The website for this book; download images used here and submit questions to the author.

www.planetphotoshop.com
Superb Photoshop resource with news and tutorials.

www.photoshopdisasters.com
Even the professionals get it wrong sometimes.

www.adobeforums.com
Adobe's own user-to-user forums.

www.worth1000.com
The world's leading Photoshop contest site.

www.photoshopgurus.com
Another large community of users with lots of helpful hints and tutorials.

ACKNOWLEDGMENTS

Thanks to Claire for her patience, understanding and unwavering support in all I do.
The photographs used in the examples and screenshots were supplied by iStockphoto, Photodisk/Getty Images, Apple Computers and the author. Photograph on page 2 (and repeated on page 118) by Julian Cornish Trestrail.